Fiesta Mexicali

Simple Mexican Cuisine with an American Twist

by Kelley Cleary Coffeen

Photography by Christopher Marchetti

NORTHLAND PUBLISHING

I dedicate this book to my darling children, Brooke and Daniel.
I wrote this book for you to show you that
anything is possible through persistence and prayer.

—KELLEY COFFEEN

Text © 2002 by Kelley Coffeen
Photographs © 2002 by Northland Publishing
All rights reserved.

www.northlandbooks.com

All toasts reprinted, by permission, from *Toasts*,
© 1981, 1991 by Paul Dickson

Composed in the United States of America
Printed in China

Edited by Tammy Gales
Designed by Lanie Schwichtenberg
Production supervised by Donna Boyd

FIRST IMPRESSION
ISBN 10: 0-87358-805-3
ISBN 13: 978-0-87358-805-8

06 07 08 09   7 6 5 4

Library of Congress Cataloging-in-Publication Data
Coffeen, Kelley
Fiesta Mexicali / by Kelley Coffeen
p. cm.
Includes bibliographical references and index.
1. Cookery, American—Southwestern style. 2. Cookery, Mexican. 3.
Cookery—Mexico—Mexicali. I. Title

TX715.2.S69 C639 2002
641.5979—dc21   2001058651

Contents

Introduction

When I was in high school, my friends and I didn't go out for a burger after school—we'd go out and grab a burrito. For our high school fund-raisers, we didn't sell candy or hold car washes, we held "Nacho-athons" (Tracy and I ate 36 each, topped with sizzling jalapeños) and sold Mexican Chicken Torta sandwiches on bolillos. Now that was fun!

I have lived and loved, eaten and celebrated from the beaches of San Diego to the hill country of Austin, from the high desert of southern New Mexico to the canyonlands of central Arizona. And even though the food might change a bit from place to place, every Southwestern celebration has always been filled with gracious hospitality and a creative and exciting atmosphere. The American West has become a culinary hot spot for enter-tainment and fun!

I like food with a little kick, and tradition with a twang. It doesn't matter whether people are watching my television segment, attending my block parties or fiestas, or reading or cooking from one of my books—I want them to be having fun. That's what I'm about, that's what my food is about, and that is what *Fiesta Mexicali* is all about.

Growing up along the Mexican border has taught me to understand and appreciate the Mexican culture and its festive cuisine. In *Fiesta Mexicali*, I have taken the rich cultural influence of our neighbors and elevated it to a whole new level of cooking. *Mexicali* fare is fun and casual, light, fiery fresh, and exciting. I keep everything good about traditional Mexican cuisine—the one-dish meal, the meat serving as just an accent, the food wrap, the ingre-dients, and the spices, and I infuse a reverence for freshness, ingenuity, and intrigue from the California kitchen. The end result of this culinary fusion is an amazing fiesta of flavors.

That's right, it's a "fiesta of flavors," a party waiting to happen. This unique cuisine is perfect for entertaining, so *Fiesta Mexicali* is the perfect entertainment cookbook! I have filled it with a selection of tantalizing cocktails, spicy salsas, snappy appetizers, and light cuisine. *Fiesta Mexicali* recipes burst with color and fun. I also offer time-saving tips on "doctoring-up" store bought foods with fresh ingredients. You see, I believe that a host should be able to go to her own party. In saying this, I am a great believer in taking shortcuts afforded by the better-quality prepared ingredients. Some of the best eating around starts with a prepared food and ends with the sort of customizing that I use liberally in my recipes. Roasted Red Pepper and Basil Cheese Round (page 27), for example, or Green Chile Chicken Alfredo (page 65), for another, are made with freshly prepared sauces from the dairy case in your grocery store. So make life a little easier and use these quality prepared products. You'll be glad you did.

Perhaps the most appealing aspect of *Fiesta Mexicali* is its reliance on economy without compromising on food appeal. This places *Fiesta Mexicali's* recipes exactly where they'll do best—affordable enough to be everyday fare and interesting enough to be special-occasion fare. Entertaining *Mexicali*-style means keeping things simple and paying close attention to detail. I want my guests to know that their friendship is worth the important little touches that make a casual get-together an event to remember. And because we are all so busy and rushed, I have even included a few fun ideas that I call "Grocery Store Décor," creative tips for your table that you can find in your local market while you are gathering your ingredients for a *Fiesta Mexicali* feast. A simple combination of plants, flowers, and produce will make your table more festive. These creative tips and details will pull your gathering together without making demands on your time or money.

So join me on this culinary adventure that embraces light and healthy eating as well as quick and easy preparation. This is your invitation to discover *Fiesta Mexicali*, the perfect collection of Mexican food recipes for the American lifestyle.

Essentials

As you glance through the recipes in this book, you will notice that certain ingredients keep coming up. You'll see fresh green chiles, tequila, a variety of cheeses, and tortillas over and over again. That's why I have added this section describing the most common ingredients you will be using.

New Mexico (Anaheim) Green Chiles
Fresh Corn Tortillas
Fresh Flour Tortillas
Asadero Cheese
Monterey Jack Cheese
Cheddar Cheese
Queso Añejo
Vine-Ripened Tomatoes
Fresh Garlic
Fresh Tomatillos
Fresh Cilantro
Fresh Lemons
Fresh Limes
Kosher Salt
Blanco Tequila
Gold Tequila
Resposado Tequila
Añejo Tequila

Chiles

There is so much debate in New Mexico about whether one's personal preference is for red or green chiles that a few years ago, the New Mexico legislature actually added this issue as an official state question (along with the official state bird, flower, etc.). "Red or Green?" slogans on bumper stickers and billboards were seen statewide, such an action by the legislature certainly demonstrates the importance of the chile crop, both economically and socially, to our state. But their popularity is not just limited to New Mexico; both red and green chiles are dearly loved by almost everyone in the Southwest and there is a growing interest in chiles of all kinds across the globe. They are used worldwide to flavor the most basic everyday dishes, from scrambled eggs to whipped potatoes. Crushed, pureed, and powdered chiles are used to spice up cocktails, sauces, entrées, and even desserts. In any form, chiles have become the condiment of choice for those of us who yearn for a flavor that is beyond everyday cooking.

I currently live in New Mexico's Mesilla Valley, which is adjacent to Hatch, New Mexico. These two areas supply the country with some of the best tasting, quality chiles found anywhere in the world. And let me tell you, no one eats their chiles hotter than my neighbors, so I have come to know and appreciate the different levels of heat in green and red chiles. In all varieties of chile, the heat is mostly carried in the veins in what is called the capsaicin, the chile's mouth-burning compound. So by removing part or all of the seeds and veins, you can create varying levels of heat. Experiment until you find a heat level that is right for you.

When it comes to new varieties, be adventurous and try all the different chiles in your produce department. For example, I especially love the earthy flavor of the poblano chile. Fire-roasted, peeled, seeded, and sliced into quarter-inch-long strips, I consider them wonderful in soups, sauces, and as a garnish for anything grilled. Smaller chiles are usually hotter than larger ones, and red chiles are usually sweeter than green. If you're buying dried chiles, make sure that they are flexible, indicating freshness. Dried chiles such as the piquin, ancho, or chile de arbol, can be rehydrated by soaking them in hot water for 20 minutes or so. They can be added whole to various dishes or chopped and minced for a more powerful punch of heat.

New Mexico chiles, also called Anaheims, such as the Big Jim and the Sandia are what we harvest around here. Every August, in about the middle of the month, the aroma of fresh roasted green chile floats through the New Mexico air. That's when I buy my chiles fresh and freeze them for the winter. Inevitably, I always run out by May or June, so I have to use frozen chiles from the market (check my list of resources on page 117). Canned chiles will also work, but there's no better way to get that unique roasted flavor than by roasting your own (see directions on page 12). Regardless of how they are served, when you see a recipe in this book that refers to green chiles, I am talking about New Mexico green or Anaheim chiles.

At the end of our harvest, the long green chiles start to turn red, and they become sweeter and hotter. They are then either dried to be used in a chile powder or chile paste, or used to make ristras—the long, ornamental strings of red chiles tied together that are traditionally hung around front doors. (Again, check my list of resources on page 117).

Finally, if you can't find fresh or dried chiles in your area, canned chiles such as pickled jalapeños and chipotles in adobo sauce are always convenient substitutions. My recipes will occasionally call for a small amount of canned chipotle chiles in adobo sauce, so if you don't use the whole can, you can preserve the unused chiles by placing them on wax paper on a baking sheet and freezing them. Once the chiles are frozen, place one or two of them in individual plastic bags, allowing you to use small portions as needed.

Tortillas

The freshest flour and corn tortillas make cooking *Fiesta Mexicali*-style easier and add flavor to the dish, but they are not always easy to come by. Ask your grocer about the arrival time of their weekly shipment of tortillas. I have even picked up a few dozen directly from the tortilla factory itself.

If you can't find fresh corn tortillas, try this: warm the corn tortillas in a microwave oven by placing 3 or 4 tortillas at a time in a small plastic bag and heating them at 50% power for 45 to 60 seconds. They should come out warm and slightly moist, which will make them easy to work with when making tacos and other recipes. If you're serving a warm corn or flour tortilla, wrap them up in foil and heat in a conventional oven at 300 degrees for 12 to 15 minutes. Flour tortillas can also be heated on a hot ungreased griddle or over a gas flame or charcoal grill for a toasty effect.

Cheese

Many Mexican cheeses have an authentic flavor that is hard to capture anywhere else in the world. They are fresh and milky-tasting, and you can often find several to choose from in your local market. One of my favorites, Asadero, is quite popular and readily available. It melts easily and has a stringy characteristic to it. To get the same effect, you can also use an even combination of Monterey Jack and mozzarella. I use a lot of Monterey Jack cheese. It has a good, almost tart flavor that accents *Mexicali* cuisine well.

Queso añejo is another Mexican cheese that is popular along the border. It is a sharper dried cheese that is used to garnish enchiladas and tacos. I have found that Feta cheese gives much of the same flavor as queso añejo and is easy to find in your local market. Another favorite, Oaxaca, is a great melting cheese, and a good choice for quesadillas. Ranchero and Cotija are a bit tart and crumbly, and are great when sprinkled over sopas, tacos, and salads. Finally, Panela is a softer cheese that can be diced and used as a garnish or served with fresh fruit.

Tomatoes

If you are the gardening type, cultivate a good stand of homegrown tomatoes for fresh Pico de Gallo or garden salsas. Since I don't have a green thumb, I am thankful for the technology that has evolved in the growing and harvesting of fresh tomatoes! I prefer "hot house" or "vine-ripened" tomatoes, which are grown indoors year-round and taste homegrown. These tomatoes have dramatically improved my salsas and tomato-based sauces and are easily found in your local market.

Tomatillos

I just started cooking with these little Mexican tomatoes a few years ago and I love them. They have a tart, citrusy flavor that goes well in fresh or cooked salsas and sauces with chiles and onions. These firm round green tomatoes are about the size of a large cherry tomato. Buy them firm with a paper-thin husk on each one, which should be removed just before cooking.

Cilantro

This fresh green herb, also known as coriander and Chinese parsley, has such a distinctive taste that it is either loved or hated. Over the last few years, it has shown up in everything from salsa to Mexican lasagna. Being quite popular, you can find this herb in your produce section sold in bunches with the stems still on. I use cilantro not only for taste, but also for the color. It adds so much to the look of my salsas. If you are not a big fan of the flavor of cilantro but want a rich green accent color in your recipe, use Italian Parsley. It is mild in flavor but big in color.

Tequila

The mysterious spirit of Tequila is both loved and scorned around the world. I have many friends who can take one whiff of tequila and remember the exact time and place they first tasted it and decidedly hated it, and I know many others, like my brother, Chris, who are becoming tequila connoisseurs. I have found it to be an acquired taste that can take you on one cocktail adventure after another.

True Tequila imported from Mexico is made with blue agave from the agave plant. Because of Mexican government regulations, there are only two kinds of officially recognized tequila: tequila that is 100% agave azul (from the blue agave plant) and tequila that is 51% agave azul and 49% sugar. Within these two categories of official tequila, there are four classifications, which strictly deal with the age of the tequila:

1. BLANCO, SILVER, OR PLATO TEQUILA is not aged at all. It's great for your basic margarita.

2. GOLD TEQUILA (called Jovan Abocado, or young and smooth) is classified as a silver tequila to which caramel and other flavors have been added. These additions make the tequila a bit sweeter and smoother. This tequila is often used as a premium addition to margaritas and other cocktails.

3. REPOSADO, which means "to rest," is aged in oak tanks or barrels for at least 60 days. It's the preferred tequila for drinking straight or in shots.

4. AÑEJO TEQUILA is aged in barrels for one to four years. Some say it's like a fine liqueur. I think of it as a sipping tequila.

Today, there are more than 420 tequila labels on the market, so it can take some effort for any person to find their favorite. Just remember that high price does not always mean good taste; there are some great inexpensive tequilas on the market. Also, many different brands are imported to different regions of the country, so ask a knowledgeable liquor connoisseur for local recommendations on reasonably priced, high-quality tequilas.

1   2   3   4

Border Blends

Salsas are at the heart of the Mexican kitchen. If there is no salsa, it's not Mexican. I add them to everything, including dips, soups, and main course delights. As I've gotten older, I've found that my taste for salsa has changed. I am now much more adventurous in combining sweet, hot, and sour flavors. These unique combinations tend to be very versatile and go beautifully with a wide variety of appetizers and main dishes. So relax and enjoy large portions of Sweet Peach Salsa served along side a heaping basket of warm, crispy corn tortilla chips, or a sesame cracker slathered with Sweet Santa Fe Spread. These intricate salsas and rich, creamy spreads are just the beginning of a cuisine that is full of infused flavors and fun. So next time you throw a fiesta, infuse a little of your own *Mexicali* flare with these delicious border blends!

PICO DE GALLO
SWEET PEACH SALSA
LEEK AND JICAMA SALSA
PINEAPPLE SALSA
MANZANA SALSA
FIESTA TOMATO RELISH
FIESTA TACO SALSA
FIESTA TABLE SALSA
FRESH SALSA VERDE
FIESTA VERDE SAUCE
MARINATED GREEN CHILE RELISH
AVOCADO TOSSA
FIERY CITRUS SALSA
BRUSCHETTA OLÉ SALSA &
PARMESAN PITA CHIPS
SPREAD SIMPATICO
CHA CHA SPREAD
SWEET SANTA FE SPREAD
PICANTE CRAB SPREAD
QUESO FUNDIDO
QUESO AMERICANA
QUESO BLANCO Y ARTICHOKES
FIESTA GUACAMOLE
CHORIZO FRIJOLES

Pico de Gallo

✸

Pico de Gallo literally means "Rooster's Beak."
Some say the name comes from the similarity
of the chopping sound of the cook's knife to
the pecking sound of a rooster. No matter
what the significance is, though, these flavors
capture the true essence of Mexico. Not only
does this salsa add color, texture, and spice
to anything you serve, but the fresh and tangy
flavor also works as an excellent chip dip.
This salsa is *muy picante*, "very spicy!"
(Makes 2 cups, enough for 4 to 6 servings)

4 TO 6 VINE-RIPENED TOMATOES, SEEDED AND CHOPPED

2 TO 3 JALAPEÑO CHILES, SEEDED AND CHOPPED

2 SERRANO CHILES, SEEDED AND CHOPPED

1 LARGE YELLOW ONION, CHOPPED

4 GREEN ONIONS, FINELY CHOPPED

2 TABLESPOONS FRESH CILANTRO, CHOPPED

JUICE OF 2 LIMES

SALT TO TASTE

Gently combine the tomato, chiles, onions,
and cilantro. Add the lime juice and the salt,
mix well, and refrigerate, stirring occasionally.
Refrigerate for at least 1 hour.

Sweet Peach Salsa

✸

Remember when our mothers and grand-
mothers made apple and peach jellies and
jams? Well, we "Millennium Moms" are waiting
for the same fruit to ripen each season, only
we are turning it into incredible salsas. This
sweet-hot salsa is a takeoff on the classic Pico
de Gallo. (Makes 2 cups, enough for 4 to 6 servings)

6 PEACHES, PITTED, PEELED, AND DICED

1 MEDIUM RED ONION, DICED

JUICE OF 2 LIMES

1 RED BELL PEPPER, DICED

2 FRESH JALAPEÑO CHILES, DICED

½ CUP JICAMA, PEELED AND CHOPPED

Gently combine all ingredients and chill for 1
hour, stirring gently and often. Serve as a
condiment with chicken, pork, or fish. It also
tastes great with warm crispy corn chips.

Leek and Jicama Salsa

This is more of a garnish than a salsa, but it is so good on so many different foods that I don't like to team it with just a single entrée or appetizer. It is especially good with Baja Tacos (page 56) or my Red Chile Carnitas (page 67). (Makes 2 cups, enough for 6 to 8 servings)

1 LEEK, WASHED AND THINLY SLICED
1 CUP JICAMA, SHREDDED
JUICE OF 5 LEMONS
1 MEDIUM RED ONION, THINLY SLICED

Combine all ingredients, mixing well. Chill for several hours, stirring occasionally to make sure that the lemon juice is absorbed.

Pineapple Salsa

This sweet and spicy salsa has a unique flavorful combination that you won't forget. It goes especially well with my Green Chile Wontons (page 35). (Makes 2 cups, enough for 4 to 6 servings)

¼ CUP RED ONION, MINCED
1 LARGE JALAPEÑO CHILE, MINCED
2 OR 3 GREEN ONIONS, MINCED, MOSTLY THE GREEN ENDS
¼ CUP RED BELL PEPPER, MINCED
½ MEDIUM-SIZED FRESH PINEAPPLE, PEELED, CORED, AND MINCED

Combine all ingredients and chill until ready to serve.

Manzana Salsa

This salsa is a refreshing chip dipper, but wait until you taste it with my Classic Carnitas (page 66). It's sort of a crazy Mexican twist on pork chops with applesauce.
(Makes about 2½ cups, enough for 4 to 6 servings)

2 LARGE GRANNY SMITH APPLES, PEELED, SEEDED, AND MINCED
1 TABLESPOON CILANTRO, MINCED
1 TABLESPOON FRESH LEMON JUICE
2 RED BELL PEPPERS, SEEDED AND CHOPPED
1 MEDIUM YELLOW ONION, FINELY CHOPPED
3 FRESH JALAPEÑO CHILES, SEEDED AND MINCED
2 TEASPOONS SALT
½ CUP APPLE JUICE

Gently toss the apple, cilantro, bell pepper, onion, lemon juice, and jalapeño in a medium bowl. Add the salt and the apple juice, and refrigerate for 1 to 2 hours before serving.

Fiesta Tomato Relish

This is more of an Americanized dip than a true salsa. My Mom used to whip up this salsa to go with grilled steaks. The next day, my girlfriends and I would top saltines with a slice of Monterey Jack cheese and a big spoonful of the remaining salsa. It was Heaven! (Makes about 2 cups, enough for 4 to 6 servings)

3 TO 4 RIPE TOMATOES, CORED AND CHOPPED

½ CUP FRESH GREEN CHILES, ROASTED, PEELED, AND CHOPPED

1 WHITE ONION, CHOPPED

2 GREEN ONIONS, CHOPPED

SALT TO TASTE

Combine the tomatoes, chile, and onion in a medium bowl. Add the green onions and salt. Mix well, and refrigerate at least 1 hour.

Fiesta Taco Salsa

One of my favorite "Taco Takeouts" has an intriguing taco sauce that I have been trying to duplicate for years. The secret ingredient turns out to be Mexican oregano, which you can get in the Mexican spice section at the market. It has a very distinctive flavor that you won't forget. My neighbor tasted it and swears there is a little taco shop in Monterey that has the same sauce. It is delicious! (Makes 5 to 6 cups, enough for 8 to 10 servings)

1 MEDIUM ONION, MINCED

1 TABLESPOON MEXICAN OREGANO

1 TABLESPOON GARLIC, MINCED

1 CAN (28 OUNCES) TOMATOES, CRUSHED OR DICED

1 CAN (15 OUNCES) TOMATO SAUCE

2 CUPS WATER

1 TABLESPOON KOSHER SALT

2 TABLESPOONS CRUSHED RED PEPPER FLAKES

Thoroughly combine all ingredients. Pulse in a blender or food processor for 5 to 8 seconds. Chill overnight before serving. Serve with tacos or quesadillas.

Directions for Roasting Chiles

Place 6 to 8 large, fresh chiles over a gas flame or a preheated outdoor grill. Turn the chiles so that all surfaces of the skins are lightly charred. Immediately place them in a paper or plastic bag, and close the bag. When the chiles have cooled, peel away the charred skins (don't wash them away or you'll lose the flavorful oils), and remove the stems and seeds.

Fiesta Table Salsa

A lot of people make their salsa differently each time. But every time Donna, my Arizona cooking pal, serves this salsa, it tastes exactly as I remembered it. This is her tried and true table salsa. Serve it chunky or pulse it in the blender or food processor for a smoother texture. (Makes 2½ to 3 cups, enough for 6 to 8 servings)

1 CAN (28 OUNCES) TOMATO CHUNKS,
PEELED AND DICED

½ CUP GREEN CHILES, ROASTED,
PEELED, AND CHOPPED

1 MEDIUM WHITE ONION, FINELY CHOPPED

1 TABLESPOON CRUSHED RED PEPPER FLAKES

1 CLOVE GARLIC, MINCED

3 TO 4 GREEN ONIONS, CHOPPED

SALT TO TASTE

Gently combine all the ingredients in a large bowl, and chill for at least 2 hours. If you would prefer a smoother texture, pour the combined ingredients into a blender or food processor and pulse for a few seconds. Serve on grilled meats or as a topping for almost anything.

Fresh Salsa Verde

I love this summer salsa. The raw tomatillos give it an almost citrusy bite, and it makes a fun dipping sauce for tacos and chips. Drop a spoonful in your tortilla soup or frijoles, or drizzle it across your grilled fish fillets. Mmmm. (Makes 2 cups, enough for 4 to 6 servings)

12 TOMATILLOS, PEELED, CORED, AND CHOPPED

1 TO 2 CLOVES GARLIC, PEELED

1 SMALL BUNCH CILANTRO, MINCED

6 GREEN ONIONS, CHOPPED

3 FRESH JALAPEÑO CHILES, SEEDED AND CHOPPED

½ TEASPOON KOSHER SALT

1 RIPE AVOCADO, CUBED (OPTIONAL)

Place the tomatillos, garlic, cilantro, green onions, jalapeños, and salt in a blender or food processor and pulse until the onions are processed, about 10 to 15 seconds. Pulse a few more times if needed, but do not process until completely smooth. Pour into an airtight container, and chill for 1 to 2 hours to allow the flavors to blend. Before serving, add the avocado cubes, if desired.

Directions for Roasting Bell Peppers

Place the bell peppers over the flame of a gas burner or over a preheated outdoor grill. Turn the peppers so that all surfaces of the skins are lightly charred. You can also place them on a baking sheet and broil them in the oven, turning every few minutes. Immediately place them in a paper or plastic bag, and close the bag. When the peppers have cooled, peel away the charred skins (don't wash them away or you'll lose the flavorful oils), and remove the stems and seeds.

Fiesta Verde Sauce

✸

Some restaurants in New Mexico heat their salsas and serve them with warm chips. I enjoy that warmth, especially during the winter. (Makes about 2½ cups, enough for 6 to 8 servings)

15 TOMATILLOS, PEELED, CORED, AND QUARTERED
3 TO 4 CLOVES GARLIC, PEELED AND MINCED
2 TABLESPOONS OLIVE OIL
3 SERRANO CHILES, SEEDED AND CHOPPED
1 TEASPOON KOSHER SALT

Place the tomatillos in a blender, and pulse for 10 to 15 seconds until they are blended but not pureed*. Sauté the garlic in the oil in a medium skillet, add the chiles, and cook until soft. Add the tomatillos and the salt, and simmer over medium heat for 8 to 10 minutes.

*You can also puree this sauce in a blender to create a "designer sauce," which makes a tasty background for Chile-Rubbed Shrimp (page 63) or a grilled steak. Simply pour the pureed sauce into a squeeze bottle, and make designs on plates before placing the entrée on top, or add a quick zigzag design across a breast of chicken or a burrito.

Marinated Green Chile Relish

✸

Weesie, Liney, and Polly, sisters who grew up on the edge of the Sonoran desert, have served this tasty relish for years, and I personally garnish my grilled rib eye steaks with this versatile relish. Or, try a triscuit with a dab of cream cheese topped with this chile, and you will make it again and again. (Makes 2 cups, enough for 4 to 6 servings)

1½ POUNDS FRESH GREEN CHILES, ROASTED,
PEELED, SEEDED, AND SLICED INTO STRIPS
¼ CUP OLIVE OIL
1 TEASPOON OREGANO
6 TO 8 CLOVES FRESH GARLIC, CHOPPED
KOSHER SALT TO TASTE

Place a 1-inch layer of chiles on the bottom of a 1-quart jar (for which you have a lid). Drizzle with 1 tablespoon of the olive oil. Sprinkle with oregano, garlic, and salt. Repeat three more times. Cover the jar with the lid, and refrigerate overnight before serving.

Avocado Tossa

✺

This isn't exactly a salsa, but you toss it with a Pico de Gallo mixture, so I call it a Tossa. I serve this Tossa with crispy hot corn tortilla chips, on grilled burgers, and with steak.
(Makes 3 cups, enough for 4 to 6 servings)

2 YELLOW CHILES, SEEDED AND MINCED

1 FRESH JALAPEÑO CHILE, SEEDED AND MINCED

5 VINE-RIPENED TOMATOES, SEEDED AND CHOPPED

1 TABLESPOON CILANTRO, MINCED

JUICE OF 3 MEDIUM LIMES

4 OR 5 LARGE AVOCADOS, PEELED, SEEDED, AND CUBED

SALT AND FRESHLY GROUND BLACK PEPPER TO TASTE

Combine the yellow chiles, jalapeño, tomatoes, cilantro, and lime juice in a large bowl. Stir until well blended. Place the avocado cubes on top, and sprinkle lightly with salt and pepper. Gently toss, and serve immediately.

Fiery Citrus Salsa

✺

Citrus and chile seem to complement each other, but in an unusual way, so you'll just have to try this salsa to know what I mean. This flavorful salsa is perfect for chicken and fish, or for any grilled meat. It also transforms Grilled Tuna Steak Tacos (page 54) into a culinary delight.
(Makes 1½ cups, enough for 4 to 6 servings)

5 TO 6 MEDIUM NAVEL ORANGES,

SKIN AND WHITE PITH REMOVED

4 LIMES, SKIN AND WHITE PITH REMOVED

1 FRESH JALAPEÑO CHILE, SEEDED AND CHOPPED

2 TEASPOONS WHITE ONION, FINELY CHOPPED

Cut the oranges and limes into small chunks, add the jalapeño and onion, mix, and chill for at least 1 hour. Stir occasionally. Use as directed in Grilled Tuna Steak Tacos or in other recipes.

Bruschetta Olé Salsa & Parmesan Pita Chips

It's Mexican! No, it's Italian! Ah, it's a little of each. This rich, robust salsa has a distinct Mexican/Italian flavor, brimming with the tantalizing taste of fresh garlic and tomato. It's a garlicky sweet relish that gets its kick from the fresh roasted green chiles. Scoop it on Parmesan Pita Chips, or pile it high on a corn tortilla chip laced with cream cheese. (Salsa makes 2½ cups, enough for 4 to 6 servings)

1 CUP GREEN CHILES, ROASTED, PEELED, AND CHOPPED

3 TO 4 VINE-RIPENED TOMATOES, SEEDED AND CHOPPED

3 CLOVES GARLIC, MINCED

1 TABLESPOON OLIVE OIL

PINCH OF KOSHER SALT

PARMESAN PITA CHIPS

Gently combine the chiles, tomatoes, garlic, and olive oil in a medium bowl. Cover and chill for 2 hours. Serve in a festive bowl with Parmesan Pita Chips.

Parmesan Pita Chips

6 PITA BREADS

2 TABLESPOONS OLIVE OIL

3 TABLESPOONS FRESHLY GRATED PARMESAN CHEESE

Preheat oven to 325°F. Line two baking sheets with parchment paper or foil. Halve each pita horizontally and brush the inside of each round with the olive oil. Cut each round into 4 wedges and place the wedges oil side up on the baking sheets. Bake about 10 minutes until crisp and brown, and sprinkle with the Parmesan cheese. Cool before serving. (Makes 48 chips)

Spread Simpatico

This is a crazy little munchy that I found a few years ago at an upscale eatery in Scottsdale, Arizona. The whipped cream cheese that you can buy in the dairy case adds a texture that makes this spread interesting. Serve it with long, thick pretzels and sesame sticks.
(Makes about 1½ cups, enough for 4 to 6 servings)

12 OUNCES WHIPPED CREAM CHEESE
½ CUP PREPARED "HOT" SALSA
2 GREEN ONIONS, MINCED

Combine the cheese and salsa, and beat with an electric mixer at medium speed for 2 to 3 minutes. Fold in the onions, cover, and chill for 1 hour to allow the flavors to blend.

Cha Cha Spread

The combination of chiles and pecans in this delicious spread defines the southern New Mexico agricultural area. Our local growers harvest the finest green chiles and pecans in the world. It is a real treat to be able to bring them together in this simple cocktail spread.
(Makes about 1½ cups, enough for 4 to 6 servings)

8 OUNCES CREAM CHEESE, AT ROOM TEMPERATURE
1½ CUPS SHARP CHEDDAR CHEESE, GRATED
⅓ CUP GREEN CHILES, CHOPPED
½ CUP PECANS, CHOPPED
1 CLOVE GARLIC, MINCED
COCKTAIL CRACKERS
KOSHER SALT TO TASTE

Combine the cream cheese, cheddar cheese, and green chiles in a large bowl. Mix well. Gently fold in the pecans, minced garlic, and salt. Chill for at least 2 hours. Serve with crackers.

Sweet Santa Fe Spread

✹

As I have said, I love infusing sweet and spicy flavors. In this sweet, nutty spread, it is the roasted peanuts that give it an added salty texture. I like it best served on sesame crackers. (Makes about 2½ cups, enough for 4 to 6 servings)

1 POUND CREAM CHEESE, SOFTENED
1 CAN (8 OUNCES) CRUSHED PINEAPPLE, WELL-DRAINED
½ CUP DRY ROASTED PEANUTS, CHOPPED
1 CLOVE GARLIC, MINCED
2 TEASPOONS CRUSHED RED PEPPER FLAKES

Thoroughly combine the cream cheese and pineapple, and add the peanuts, garlic, and crushed red pepper flakes. Blend well, chill for 1 hour, and serve with cut celery or sesame cocktail crackers.

Picante Crab Spread

✹

Picante means "spicy," which is how I like this spread—with a little kick. Rich and oozing with cheese, this fun little spread gets served time and time again at my house, usually as part of an array of *antojitos*, or "little whims." If you prefer less of a kick than I do, just reduce the quantity of crushed red pepper flakes. (Makes 3½ cups, enough for 6 to 8 servings)

8 OUNCES CREAM CHEESE, SOFTENED
½ CUP MAYONNAISE
½ CUP PARMESAN CHEESE, GRATED
1 POUND CRABMEAT, PICKED CLEAN
1 TO 2 TEASPOONS CRUSHED RED PEPPER FLAKES,
TO TASTE

Preheat the oven to 350°F. Thoroughly combine the cream cheese, mayonnaise, and all but 1 tablespoon of the Parmesan cheese in a medium bowl. Gently fold in the crabmeat and the red pepper flakes. Pour into an ovenproof serving dish, sprinkle the top with the remaining Parmesan, and bake for 20 to 25 minutes, until lightly brown and bubbly. Serve with corn tortilla chips or cocktail crackers.

Light Bites

With happy hour becoming a mainstay in America, a few bite-sized appetizers and an interesting cocktail make for an appealing way to start out the evening. *Fiesta Mexicali* offers you an array of enticing *antojitos*, which best translates as "little whims." Here, I infuse unexpected flavors and ingredients for some light and tasty appetizers. I offer you a variety of light bites to choose from, including fresh fruit marinated with chile; shellfish and seafood served in light, tangy sauces; soft flour tortillas filled with creamy, herbed cheeses; and seasoned meats mixed with fresh veggies. Take time for happy hour...a *Fiesta Mexicali* happy hour.

FRESCO DE FRUIT
MARGARITA RUMBA
RELLENO TARTS
JALAPEÑO QUICHE SQUARES
ROASTED RED PEPPER &
BASIL CHEESE ROUND
SMOKY CHIPOTLE TOSTADITAS
BLACK BEAN BRUSCHETTA
PAPPAS CON CHILE
PESTO SPIRALS
SMOKY SPIRALS
SWEET CHICKEN SPIRALS
CLASSIC GREEN CHILE SPIRALS
FRESH VEGGIE SPIRALS
FETA AND BLACK OLIVE SPIRALS
GOLDEN CHILE STRIPS
GREEN CHILE WONTONS
OYSTERS ROCKAPEPPER
CHILLED GREEN CHILE OYSTERS
STUFFED MONTEREY MUSHROOMS
CEVICHE SUPREME
SURFIN' SEAFOOD COCKTAIL
TEQUILA SHRIMP
SHRIMP SALSA CUPITAS
GRILLED PLAZA QUESADILLA
CHORIZO MUSHROOM QUESADILLA
COASTAL CRAB QUESADILLA
ROASTED GARLIC CHICKEN QUESADILLA
GARDEN QUESADILLA
PESTO CILANTRO QUESADILLA

Fresco de Fruit

I remember going to a little patio café over the border and munching on fresh fruit and jicama sprinkled with crushed red pepper flakes. One bite led to another, and I was hooked. In my version of this healthy appetizer, I like to marinate the fruit by tossing it in fresh lime juice, and then scattering crushed red pepper flakes on top of it. (Makes 4 to 6 servings)

1 FRESH PINEAPPLE, PEELED, CORED,
AND CUT INTO CHUNKS
1 JICAMA, PEELED AND CUT INTO CHUNKS
3 TO 4 KIWI, PEELED AND CUT INTO CHUNKS
JUICE OF 3 LIMES
ZEST OF 1 ORANGE
8 OUNCES FRESH RASPBERRIES
2 TEASPOONS CRUSHED RED PEPPER FLAKES
FRUIT PLATTER DIPPING SAUCE (SEE RECIPE BELOW)

Gently toss the pineapple, jicama, and kiwi with fresh lime juice and orange zest in a large bowl. Arrange the fruit on a serving platter, leaving space in the middle for a bowl of dipping sauce. Scatter the fresh raspberries around the platter, and sprinkle the crushed red pepper flakes evenly over the fruit. Make the dipping sauce. Chill until ready to serve.

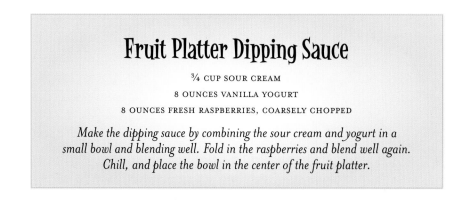

Fruit Platter Dipping Sauce

¾ CUP SOUR CREAM
8 OUNCES VANILLA YOGURT
8 OUNCES FRESH RASPBERRIES, COARSELY CHOPPED

Make the dipping sauce by combining the sour cream and yogurt in a small bowl and blending well. Fold in the raspberries and blend well again. Chill, and place the bowl in the center of the fruit platter.

Margarita Rumba

Originally, I created this fruit salad more for the look than the taste. Luckily, I got both. This is a showstopper—fresh fruit chunks glazed in a zesty margarita flavor and served in a glass bowl or trifle dish rimmed with margarita salt. (Makes 8 to 10 servings)

½ CUP PREPARED MARGARITA MIX

1 OUNCE ORANGE-FLAVORED LIQUEUR, SUCH AS TRIPLE SEC, COINTREAU, OR GRAND MARNIER

2 TABLESPOONS HONEY

3 FRESH MEDIUM-SIZED PINEAPPLES,TRIMMED, CORED, AND CUT INTO 1-INCH CHUNKS

6 KIWIS, PEELED AND CUT INTO ½-INCH CHUNKS

3 QUARTS STRAWBERRIES, STEMS REMOVED, QUARTERED

2 POUNDS RED SEEDLESS GRAPES, RINSED

ZEST AND JUICE OF 3 LIMES

ZEST AND JUICE OF 1 LEMON

1 CUP KOSHER SALT

Combine the margarita mix, liqueur, and honey. Blend well. Gently combine the fruit in a large bowl.

One hour before serving, sprinkle the lime and lemon zests over the fruit (be sure to wash the lemons and limes before removing the zest), and pour the margarita glaze over the fruit. Add the juice of the lemon and limes. Mix gently until all fruit has been coated. Chill for 30 minutes, stirring every 10 minutes so the fruit absorbs the flavors.

Pour the salt on a large plate or flat surface. Prepare the serving bowl by rubbing the rim with the juiced lemon or lime halves and then dipping the moistened rim in the salt. Shake off the excess salt. Gently spoon the fruit into the serving bowl, taking care not to disturb the rim.

Relleno Tarts

◎

This is one of my favorite *antojitos*! They're little bites of chile and cheese, reminiscent of the classic chile relleno—a green chile stuffed with cheese, dipped in an egg batter, and fried. You can make these tarts ahead of time and freeze them, or serve them fresh out of the oven. (Makes 36 pieces)

NON-STICK COOKING SPRAY

4 TABLESPOONS LIGHTLY SALTED BUTTER

1 CUP SMALL-CURD COTTAGE CHEESE

5 EGGS

¼ CUP FLOUR

½ TEASPOON BAKING POWDER

½ TEASPOON SALT

½ CUP GREEN CHILE, MINCED

10 OUNCES MONTEREY JACK CHEESE, SHREDDED

Spray a mini-muffin pan. Preheat oven to 350°F. Melt the butter in a large bowl, and let cool for 10 minutes. Add the cottage cheese, and then the eggs. In a small bowl, combine the flour, baking powder, and salt. Add the dry ingredients to the egg mixture. Fold in the chile and the shredded cheese. Mix well. Spoon 1 tablespoon of the mixture into each muffin tin, and bake for 10 to 14 minutes, or until puffed and golden brown.

Jalapeño Quiche Squares

◎

Turn up the heat and dance to the beat! I added a bit of jalapeño chile and meat to my favorite cheeses and came up with a smashing little cocktail square. This little chile bite is a wonderful appetizer, but it can also be served at brunch as well. (Makes 6 to 8 servings)

½ POUND MILD CHEDDAR OR

LONGHORN CHEESE, GRATED

½ POUND MONTEREY JACK CHEESE, GRATED

8 STRIPS BACON, CRUMBLED,

OR 1 CUP HAM, FINELY DICED

8 EGGS, BEATEN

½ CUP WHOLE MILK

4 FRESH JALAPEÑO CHILES,

SEEDED AND MINCED

1 (8 COUNT) CAN OF CRESCENT ROLLS

Preheat oven to 350°F. Press the crescent dough across the bottom and up the sides of a 13 x 9 baking pan. Sprinkle the meat and jalapeño over the unbaked crescent dough. Combine the cheeses, and spread over the meat and jalapeño layer. Combine the eggs and the milk, and pour the mixture on top of the cheese layer. Bake for 30 to 40 minutes until the top is golden brown. Cut into 1-inch squares and serve warm.

Roasted Red Pepper & Basil Cheese Round

My girlfriend Cynthia has served this Italian-inspired showstopper at several cocktail parties, and she always gets rave reviews. The colorful cheese wedges are full of sweet basil, roasted red pepper, and roasted green chile. (Makes 6 to 8 servings)

½ POUND PROVOLONE, SLICED PAPER-THIN

8 OUNCES CREAM CHEESE, SOFTENED

5 TABLESPOONS BUTTER, SOFTENED

½ CUP PREPARED BASIL PESTO

¼ CUP PECANS, TOASTED AND CHOPPED

1 RED BELL PEPPER, ROASTED

4 OUNCES GREEN CHILE, ROASTED AND CHOPPED

¼ CUP OLIVE OIL

2 BAGUETTES, THINLY SLICED

Line a small springform pan with plastic wrap, leaving plenty of overhang on each side. Place the provolone slices on the bottom and partially up the sides of the pan, overlapping where necessary. Combine the cream cheese and the butter with a fork in a medium-sized bowl. Add the pesto and mix well. Spread one-third of the pesto mixture over the provolone. Sprinkle with one-third of the pecans, one-third of the red pepper, and one-third of the green chile. Repeat twice, and finish with a layer of provolone. Cover with plastic wrap, press down, and refrigerate for at least 12 hours. Remove from the refrigerator, and invert the cheese round onto a serving platter. Remove the plastic wrap. Slice half the round into thin wedges, and arrange the wedges on the platter around the remaining uncut cheese round. Serve at room temperature. Slice more as needed.

Lightly brush the oil on one side of each baguette slice. Place baguette slices on a baking sheet and broil 3 to 4 minutes until lightly browned. Serve with the cheese wedges.

Smoky Chipotle Tostaditas

〰

This is an upscale version of one of my childhood favorites—large platters of bite-sized tostadas slathered with a rich, spicy bean spread and topped with fresh veggies and cheese. It makes one festive appetizer. (Makes 36 tostaditas)

2 CANS (15 OUNCES EACH) BLACK BEANS

3 CHIPOTLE CHILES IN ADOBO SAUCE, MINCED

36 ROUND CORN TORTILLA CHIPS

3 CUPS LETTUCE, SHREDDED

1½ TABLESPOONS PREPARED ITALIAN DRESSING

2 CUPS CHEDDAR CHEESE, SHREDDED

2 MEDIUM TOMATOES, SEEDED AND CHOPPED

Drain the beans slightly, pour them into a medium skillet, add the chiles, and bring to a boil. After the beans have boiled for at least 2 minutes, reduce the heat and mash the beans with a potato masher. They should be well mashed but not completely smooth. Allow the bean mixture to cool for 10 to 12 minutes, and then spread 1 tablespoon of the mixture on each tortilla chip and place the chips on a serving platter. (The bean mixture should not be so warm that it makes the chips soggy.)

Toss the shredded lettuce with the Italian dressing in a medium bowl. Place 1 tablespoon of the lettuce on each bean-covered chip, and sprinkle the entire platter with the shredded cheese and chopped tomato.

Black Bean Bruschetta

〰

I can never seem to make enough of this dish, and I often find that anyone within walking distance of the kitchen hangs around it. Tangy balsamic vinegar and basil give this bean salsa a new dimension. (Makes 6 to 8 servings)

2 CANS (15 OUNCES EACH) BLACK BEANS

½ CUP OLIVE OIL

3 TABLESPOONS BALSAMIC VINEGAR

½ CUP FRESH BASIL, CHOPPED

2 CLOVES GARLIC, MINCED

¼ TEASPOON RED PEPPER FLAKES

¼ TEASPOON SALT

¼ TEASPOON FRESHLY GROUND BLACK PEPPER

1 LOAF BAGUETTE BREAD, THINLY SLICED

Rinse and drain the beans and place them in a large mixing bowl. Gently combine 6 tablespoons of the olive oil, vinegar, basil, garlic, red pepper flakes, salt, and pepper. Let sit for at least an hour, tossing occasionally. Lightly brush the remaining 2 tablespoons of olive oil on each side of each bread slice. Place the bread slices on a baking sheet and broil until lightly browned, about 3 to 4 minutes. Top each slice of bread with some of the bean mixture, and place the bread on a serving platter.

Pappas con Chile

⊙

I have eaten potato skins with almost every kind of topping baked and broiled on top, but this is one of my favorites. Try this simple combination— a double-baked crispy potato skin dipped in a light chile cream sauce. (Makes 6 to 8 servings)

6 MEDIUM POTATOES, BAKED

2 TABLESPOONS OLIVE OIL

1 TABLESPOON KOSHER SALT

LIGHT CHILE CREAM DIPPING SAUCE (SEE RECIPE BELOW)

Preheat oven to 350°F. Bake the potatoes in a preheated oven for 1 to 1½ hours until the flesh is soft when poked with a fork. Let them cool. Slice each potato in half lengthwise. Scoop out the potato flesh, and use in another recipe. Place the skins face down on a baking sheet. Brush lightly with olive oil and sprinkle with kosher salt. Turn over so they sit skin side down and brush the insides lightly with olive oil. Bake at 350°F for 10 to 15 minutes more, until the skins are crispy. Slice each piece lengthwise into quarters, and serve on a platter with a bowl of Light Chile Cream Dipping Sauce in the center.

Light Chile Cream Dipping Sauce

¾ CUP SOUR CREAM

¼ CUP HEAVY CREAM

½ CUP GREEN CHILE, ROASTED, SEEDED, AND CHOPPED

2 CLOVES GARLIC, MINCED

¼ CUP ONION, CHOPPED

1 TABLESPOON GRANULATED CHICKEN BOUILLON

Place all ingredients into a blender or food processor and pulse for 10 to 20 seconds, checking to see that all ingredients are well blended. Pour the mixture into a serving bowl, and use as directed in the preceding recipe. (Makes about 1 ½ cups)

Spirals

My sister-in-law, JoJo, who is a natural party planner, started me on these time-saving appetizers years ago. Soft flour tortillas rolled up with different cream fillings and cut into lovely spirals can be made and frozen a few days before your gathering. They are my *Fiesta Mexicali* version of miniature tea sandwiches. Create your own flavors and tasty combinations. The following variations are just some of my favorites.

To make spirals, follow the directions below, substituting ingredients unique to each recipe where necessary. (Recipes make 4 to 6 servings)

Combine all the ingredients with the cream cheese in a medium-sized mixing bowl. Using 2 tablespoons per tortilla, spread the mixture to the outer edge of each tortilla, covering the full surface. Roll up tightly, making sure each tortilla ends up as an even, round tube shape. Place the rolled tortillas in a large resealable plastic bag or plastic wrap, and refrigerate for up to a day or freeze for longer. Before serving, slice into ¼-inch rounds and arrange on a platter.

Pesto Spirals

8 OUNCES CREAM CHEESE, SOFTENED
1 PACKAGE (5 OUNCES) DRY PESTO SAUCE MIX
1 TABLESPOON RED BELL PEPPER, MINCED
2 TABLESPOONS SOUR CREAM
4 (10- TO 12-INCH) FLOUR TORTILLAS

Smoky Spirals

8 OUNCES CREAM CHEESE
2 PICKLED JALAPEÑO CHILES, MINCED
2 SLICES HICKORY-SMOKED BACON,
COOKED AND FINELY CRUMBLED
4 (10- TO 12-INCH) FLOUR TORTILLAS

Sweet Chicken Spirals

8 OUNCES CREAM CHEESE
4 TO 6 OUNCES COOKED WHITE
CHICKEN MEAT, FINELY SHREDDED*
1 TABLESPOON APRICOT JELLY
1 GREEN ONION, MINCED
4 (10- TO 12-INCH) FLOUR TORTILLAS

*Place 1 (4 to 6) ounce chicken breast in a medium sized saucepan half full of water. Bring to a boil. Boil for 8 to 10 minutes until done all the way through. Cool on a cutting board and shred with a fork.

Classic Green Chile Spirals

◎

8 OUNCES CREAM CHEESE

4 OUNCES GREEN CHILE, ROASTED,

SEEDED, AND CHOPPED

1 CLOVE GARLIC, MINCED

PINCH OF KOSHER SALT

4 (10- TO 12-INCH) FLOUR TORTILLAS

Fresh Veggie Spirals

◎

8 OUNCES CREAM CHEESE

1 GREEN ONION, MINCED

2 TABLESPOONS FRESH RED BELL PEPPER, MINCED

1 TABLESPOON CARROT, GRATED

2 FRESH JALAPEÑO CHILES, SEEDED AND MINCED

PINCH OF KOSHER SALT

4 (10- TO 12-INCH) FLOUR TORTILLAS

Feta and Black Olive Spirals

◎

4 OUNCES FETA CHEESE

2 TABLESPOONS BLACK OLIVES, MINCED

8 OUNCES CREAM CHEESE

4 (10- TO 12-INCH) FLOUR TORTILLAS

Making Spirals

Combine all the ingredients with the cream cheese in a medium-sized mixing bowl.

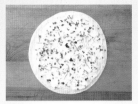

Using 2 tablespoons per tortilla, spread the mixture to the outer edge of each tortilla, covering the full surface.

Roll up tightly, making sure each tortilla ends up as an even, round tube shape. Place the rolled tortillas in a large resealable plastic bag or plastic wrap, and refrigerate for up to a day or freeze for longer.

Before serving, slice into ¼-inch rounds and arrange on a platter.

Substitute ingredients unique to each recipe where necessary.
(All recipes make 4 to 6 servings)

Golden Chile Strips

East meets West with these zesty green chile strips wrapped in a golden batter. Every time I serve this unusual appetizer I get compliments, not only for taste but also on the idea of infusing these two types of cuisine. The Asian dipping sauce adds a unique flavor to this Southwestern favorite. (Makes 4 to 6 servings)

1 CUP FLOUR

½ TEASPOON SALT

½ TEASPOON BAKING SODA

½ CUP WATER

2 EGG WHITES, WHIPPED

VEGETABLE OIL

10 TO 12 FRESH GREEN CHILES, ROASTED,

PEELED, SEEDED CAREFULLY SO THAT THE STEMS ARE STILL

ATTACHED, AND DRIED ON PAPER TOWELS*

ORIENTAL DIPPING SAUCE

AND/OR HONEY TERIYAKI DIPPING SAUCE

(SEE RECIPES ON FOLLOWING PAGE)

Make a batter by combining the flour, salt, and baking soda in a large bowl, adding the water, mixing well, and folding in the egg whites. Meanwhile, place 2 to 3 inches of oil in a large skillet or deep fryer over medium-high heat. Dip each chile in batter, and then deep-fry it, turning occasionally until golden brown. Cool slightly before serving. Serve with Oriental Dipping Sauce and/or Honey Teriyaki Dipping Sauce.

*You may substitute canned whole chiles that have been rinsed and dried with a paper towel.

Oriental Dipping Sauce

¼ CUP SOY SAUCE

2 TABLESPOONS HEAVY CREAM

1 CLOVE MINCED GARLIC

Combine all ingredients. Chill until ready to serve.
(Makes 4 servings)

Honey Teriyaki Dipping Sauce

¼ CUP TERIYAKI

2 TABLESPOONS HONEY

2 GREEN ONIONS, CHOPPED

Combine all ingredients. Serve at room temperature.
(Makes 4 servings)

Green Chile Wontons

An innovative restaurateur introduced me to Green Chile Wontons a few years back. Buddy Ritter has a way of infusing our Mexican cuisine with various cultures from around the world. This *antojito* has become a favorite in the Southwest. (Makes 24 pieces, or 4 to 6 servings)

¼ POUND CHEDDAR CHEESE, SHREDDED

¼ POUND MONTEREY JACK CHEESE, SHREDDED

½ CUP HOT GREEN CHILES, DICED

½ TEASPOON SALT

¼ TEASPOON BLACK PEPPER

¼ TEASPOON CUMIN

1 CLOVE GARLIC, FINELY CHOPPED

24 EGG-ROLL SKINS, EACH 2 X 2 INCHES

FLOUR, FOR DUSTING

VEGETABLE OIL, FOR DEEP-FRYING

PINEAPPLE SALSA, FOR DIPPING (PAGE 11)

Place the cheeses, chiles, salt, pepper, cumin, and garlic in a large mixing bowl, and toss gently. Place the egg-roll skins on a clean surface or cutting board, wet the edges with a bit of water, and place a heaping teaspoon of the cheese filling in the center of each skin. Fold into a triangle, dampen the edges, and press them together. Dust with flour, and deep-fry in 3 inches of hot vegetable oil until golden brown. Serve Pineapple Salsa on the side for dipping.

Oysters RockaPepper

Some like 'em hot, some like 'em cold. I like my oysters hot or cold—but always spicy! Don't shy away from preparing fresh oysters at home. If fresh seafood is hard to come by, special-order fresh oysters from the seafood department at your local market. Make sure they have no odor and that each one is closed. Remember that the oysters are still alive in the shell, and you want them to stay alive until you shuck them, so leave an opening in the bag while they're in your refrigerator to allow them to breathe. Here is a Mexican version of Oysters Rockefeller, broiled with a rich, creamy, spicy layer of chile and cheese. (Makes 4 to 6 servings)

2 TEASPOONS OLIVE OIL

4 CLOVES FRESH GARLIC, MINCED

3 TABLESPOONS GREEN CHILE, ROASTED,
PEELED, AND CHOPPED

2 TABLESPOONS RED BELL PEPPER, ROASTED,
SEEDED, PEELED, AND CHOPPED

PINCH OF KOSHER SALT

½ POUND MONTEREY JACK CHEESE, GRATED

12 TO 16 FRESH OYSTERS ON THE HALF SHELL*

Heat the olive oil in a small skillet for about 2 minutes over medium heat. Sauté the garlic in the oil for 1 to 2 minutes, then add the green chile, bell pepper, and salt. Sauté for 2 to 3 minutes more, remove from the heat, and let cool to room temperature. Place mixture in a medium bowl with the grated cheese, and mix well. Remove the oysters on the half shells from the refrigerator and place them on an ovenproof platter. Top each oyster with a heaping teaspoon of the cheese mixture. Broil for 6 to 8 minutes, or until the cheese is bubbly and lightly browned. Serve immediately.

*You can ask your fishmonger to shuck the oysters and save the shells. Or, if you prefer to do it yourself, rinse the outside of each closed shell, and wash away any dirt and loose shell. Find a small opening in the shell, usually at the narrow end, and place your shucking tool (a small, clean screwdriver will work) in the opening, and pop open the shell. Carefully remove any dirt or shell fragments. Place on a platter and chill for at least 1 hour.

Chilled Green Chile Oysters

🌀

I like to put salsa on just about everything, and oysters are no exception. You'll go wild for these fresh oysters on the half shell. They make a festive, cool appetizer from the deep blue sea. (Makes 4 to 6 servings)

¼ CUP GREEN CHILE, ROASTED,
PEELED, SEEDED, AND CHOPPED
1 TABLESPOON RED BELL PEPPER, ROASTED,
SEEDED, PEELED, AND CHOPPED
2 CLOVES FRESH GARLIC, MINCED
JUICE OF 2 MEDIUM LEMONS
12 TO 16 FRESH OYSTERS ON THE HALF SHELL*
2 MEDIUM LEMONS, CUT INTO WEDGES

Toss the chile, bell pepper, garlic, and lemon juice together in a small mixing bowl. Remove the chilled oysters on the half shell from the refrigerator and arrange them on a serving platter. Top each oyster with a heaping teaspoon of relish, and serve with lemon wedges.

*To shuck and prepare the oysters, follow the directions in the recipe note on page 36.

Stuffed Monterey Mushrooms

🌀

These little bites—tender mushrooms stuffed with a spicy cheese filling—are big on flavor. I like to use Jimmy Dean sausage, because I think it has a perfect blend of spices. (Makes 24 mushrooms, about 4 to 6 servings)

24 MEDIUM MUSHROOM CAPS
1 PACKAGE (1 POUND) SPICED SAUSAGE
8 OUNCES CREAM CHEESE
2 OUNCES MONTEREY JACK CHEESE, GRATED
1 TABLESPOON CRUSHED RED PEPPER FLAKES
2 TABLESPOONS PARMESAN CHEESE, GRATED

Wash the mushrooms and pat dry with paper towels. Remove the stems and set aside (they can be minced and added to the sausage mixture later if desired). Preheat the oven to 350°F. Cook the sausage in a large skillet until done, drain, and place in a mixing bowl. Add the cream cheese, Monterey Jack cheese, and crushed red pepper flakes. Mix well. Place 1 heaping teaspoon of the mixture into each mushroom cap. Place the stuffed mushroom caps on a rimmed baking pan, sprinkle with Parmesan, and bake for 20 minutes. Remove from oven and let cool for 5 minutes. Serve stuffed mushrooms on a decorative serving platter.

Ceviche Supreme

Splashes of red, green, and yellow teamed with a delicate, white seafood make ceviche (pronounced se-VI-chee) an exotic appetizer. The combination of chile, lime, and fish conveys the authentic flavors of Mexico and the West coast, and in one of the miracles of the kitchen, the citric acid actually cooks the fish without heat. Make sure to use very fresh fish. Fill a martini glass with this colorful delicacy, garnish with tortilla chips, and watch your guests go wild. (Makes 4 to 6 servings)

1 POUND FRESH HALIBUT, CUT IN ¼-INCH CUBES

JUICE OF 10 FRESH LIMES

1 WHITE ONION, FINELY CHOPPED

4 TO 6 FIRM, VINE-RIPENED TOMATOES, PEELED, SEEDED, AND CHOPPED

1 FRESH JALAPEÑO CHILE, SEEDED AND DICED

1 FRESH SERRANO CHILE, SEEDED AND DICED

1 YELLOW CHILE, SEEDED AND DICED

GARLIC SALT TO TASTE

FRESHLY GROUND BLACK PEPPER TO TASTE

CRISP CORN TORTILLA CHIPS

Toss the fish in the lime juice and marinate in the refrigerator for 1 hour. Add the onion, tomatoes, chiles, garlic salt, and black pepper, and toss gently to combine. Chill for 2 hours more. Serve in martini glasses with tortilla chips.

Surfin' Seafood Cocktail

One blazing summer day, a friend insisted that we run across the border and get a Mexican seafood cocktail. Our adventure led to a little taco shack in a back alley in the heart of San Luis, Mexico. I will never know how she found this place, but there in the hot sun we dined on the most refreshing combination of fresh lobster, shrimp, scallops, and fresh veggies, all in a rich, spicy, tomato cocktail sauce. This is a versatile dish that you can serve in individual parfait glasses, or in a large bowl accompanied by warm crispy corn tortilla chips. (Makes 4 cocktails)

¾ POUND FRESH JUMBO SHRIMP AND 1 MEDIUM-SIZED LOBSTER TAIL*

1 CUP CELERY, CHOPPED

3 GREEN ONIONS, CHOPPED

2 TABLESPOONS FRESH CILANTRO, MINCED

1 MEDIUM VINE-RIPENED TOMATO, SEEDED AND CHOPPED

2 CANS (11.5 OUNCES) OR 3 CUPS V8 SPICY-HOT VEGETABLE JUICE

½ CUP PREPARED PICANTE-STYLE SALSA

½ TEASPOON SALT

½ TEASPOON FRESHLY GROUND BLACK PEPPER

JUICE OF 2 LIMES

1 LIME, CUT INTO 4 WEDGES

To cook the shrimp and lobster, fill a large pot ¾ full with water and bring to a boil. Carefully add the shrimp and lobster to the boiling water and cook 3 to 4 minutes until the shrimp turn pinkish orange. Remove shrimp with a slotted spoon. The lobster will take a bit longer; remove it from the pot when the flesh turns opaque. Let the shrimp and lobster cool, then remove the shells and devein the shrimp. Rinse and chop the shrimp and lobster. Cover and chill in the refrigerator.

Combine the celery, onions, cilantro, tomato, vegetable juice, and salsa in a large bowl. Add the shrimp and lobster, mix well, and season with salt, pepper, and lime juice. Chill for at least 1 hour before serving. Serve in 4 parfait glasses garnished with lime wedges.

*This recipe calls for approximately 1 pound of seafood. Select your favorites—scallops, shrimp, fresh crab, or maybe a little octopus.

Tequila Shrimp

This smooth, buttery dish is like shrimp scampi with a kick. The gold tequila, which is a bit sweet, complements the buttery sauce. Serve it as an appetizer or as an entrée over a bed of fresh pasta. (Makes 4 to 6 servings)

6 CLOVES GARLIC, CHOPPED
¼ POUND (1 STICK) BUTTER
3 OUNCES GOLD TEQUILA
PINCH OF KOSHER SALT
1½ POUNDS JUMBO SHRIMP, SHELLED,
DEVEINED, AND RINSED
JUICE OF 3 LIMES
1 TABLESPOON FRESH CILANTRO, CHOPPED
1 TABLESPOON CRUSHED RED PEPPER FLAKES (OPTIONAL)

In a large skillet, cook the garlic in 6 tablespoons of butter over medium-low heat until the garlic is soft. Add the tequila and salt, and mix until well blended. Increase the heat to medium, and add the shrimp, stirring and tossing constantly. Cook for 5 to 7 minutes until the shrimp are a bright pinkish orange and firm. To check, cut a shrimp in half at the thickest part to see if it is opaque throughout. When done, remove the shrimp from the skillet and keep warm.

Add the lime juice, cilantro, and crushed pepper, if desired, to the butter mixture, and bring to a simmer over medium heat, stirring constantly for 2 minutes. Add the remaining butter to the sauce. Return the shrimp to the butter sauce and gently toss. Serve warm with fancy toothpicks.

Shrimp Salsa Cupitas

Cilantro is to Mexican cuisine what parsley is to the American plate. Cilantro has a way of balancing the fire from those beloved chiles with the rich buttery flavor of avocado and lime in this seafood delight. (Makes 6 servings)

GARLIC-FLAVORED COOKING SPRAY

6 FRESH CORN TORTILLAS

SALT

1 POUND MEDIUM SHRIMP

1 TABLESPOON FRESH CILANTRO, MINCED

1 FRESH JALAPEÑO CHILE, SEEDED AND DICED

⅓ CUP RED ONION, DICED

2 MEDIUM AVOCADOS, RIPE BUT FIRM

JUICE OF 2 LIMES

Preheat the oven to 400°F. While the oven is heating, lightly spray a muffin pan (making 6 to 12 large muffins) with cooking spray. Place half the tortillas in a small, plastic sandwich bag, and place the open bag in the microwave at 50% power for 30 to 45 seconds. The tortillas should come out warm and moist. One at a time, spray each side of the tortillas with cooking spray, and, while the tortillas are still warm, gently form them into a cup by molding them into a muffin space. When all the tortilla cups are formed in the pan, lightly salt each one and immediately place the muffin pan in the oven. Bake for 8 to 10 minutes, until the tortillas are crisp and slightly brown. Remove from the oven and cool.

To make the salsa filling, fill a large pot ¾ full with water and bring to a boil. Carefully add the shrimp to the boiling water and cook 3 to 4 minutes until the shrimp turn pinkish orange. Remove the shrimp with a slotted spoon, and let cool. Remove shells, devein shrimp, place in a colander, rinse with cool water, and chill in the refrigerator for 1 hour. Coarsely chop the shrimp, and toss in a large bowl with the cilantro, jalapeño, and onion. Just before serving, peel the avocados, seed them, and dice them into bite-sized chunks. Add the lime juice and avocado to the salsa mixture, and toss gently. Spoon into the cupitas. For a stunning presentation, place each filled shell in a martini glass, and place the glasses on a silver serving tray.

Quesadillas

Quesadillas, cheese crisps, and toasted cheese tortillas are all variations of the Mexican grilled cheese sandwich. Since the early 1980s, they have gone from being a snack or appetizer to a main dish and are now stuffed with everything from fresh veggies to sautéed chicken and sirloin. They can be grilled, baked, broiled, or microwaved. A favorite in the Southwest is a large flour tortilla layered with a Cheddar cheese, such as longhorn, or a white cheese such as Monterey Jack or Asadero, roasted open-faced under the broiler until the edges are crispy brown, and then slathered with taco sauce and cracked black pepper. Of course, I can't stop there, so following are a few flavorful quesadillas and open-faced cheese crisps. Serve them as appetizers, or serve them for dinner!

Grilled Plaza Quesadilla

✺

This is my idea of the Mexican-American grilled cheese sandwich. The combination of chile, ham, and cheese makes a delicious filled turnover. When I get that longing for a good old grilled cheese sandwich, I whip up one of these. (Makes 4 servings)

3 (10- TO 12-INCH) FLOUR TORTILLAS
2 CUPS MILD CHEDDAR OR LONGHORN CHEESE, SHREDDED
¼ CUP RED ONION, THINLY SLICED
½ CUP GREEN CHILE, ROASTED, PEELED, AND CHOPPED
6 SLICES DELI-STYLE COOKED HAM
3 TEASPOONS BUTTER
FIESTA TACO SALSA (PAGE 12)

Lay out the tortillas, and sprinkle one-third of the cheese on each. Place one-third of the onion, chile, and ham slices on one side of each tortilla. Melt 1 teaspoon of butter before placing each quesadilla in a large skillet or on a flat griddle pan. When the butter is melted, place the tortilla on the hot surface. As the cheese begins to melt, fold the tortillas in half. Cook and turn over until the tortilla browns. Slice into thirds and serve with Fiesta Taco Salsa.

Chorizo Mushroom Quesadilla

✺

Chorizo sausage has such a unique flavor. It is considered more as a breakfast sausage in the Southwest. Chorizo and eggs, chorizo and potato burritos—these are a couple of common dishes, but I like the spicy flavor of this sausage with Monterey Jack cheese in this simple quesadilla. (Makes 4 to 6 servings)

4 OUNCES CHORIZO SAUSAGE, COOKED AND DRAINED*
½ POUND MONTEREY JACK CHEESE, GRATED
6 TO 8 FRESH MEDIUM MUSHROOMS, SLICED
4 GREEN ONIONS, CHOPPED, GREEN PART ONLY
4 (8- TO 10-INCH) FLOUR TORTILLAS
4 TEASPOONS BUTTER
FIESTA TOMATO RELISH (PAGE 12) OR
MANZANA SALSA (PAGE 11)

Spread 1 ounce of the cooked and drained chorizo on half of each tortilla. Divide the cheese, mushrooms, and green onions evenly over the tortillas. Melt 1 teaspoon of butter per quesadilla in a large skillet or on a griddle. Place each of the topped tortillas open-faced on the hot surface, and grill over medium heat for 2 to 3 minutes until the cheese starts to melt. Gently fold the tortilla in half, covering the filling. Continue grilling, turning until the tortillas are golden brown and the cheese has melted. Serve with Fiesta Tomato Relish or, for a sweet and spicy twist, with Manzana Salsa.

*Ask your grocer to order chorizo if it is hard to find.

Coastal Crab Quesadilla

Even though flour tortillas are the most common, I often wrap this crab and cheese filling in warm corn tortillas for a different flavor combination. This upscale quesadilla is simple and elegant. (Makes 4 to 6 servings)

½ POUND MONTEREY JACK CHEESE, GRATED

6 TO 8 OUNCES FRESH CRABMEAT,
CLEANED AND PICKED OVER

2 TABLESPOONS RED BELL PEPPER, MINCED

2 GREEN ONIONS, CHOPPED

10 (6-INCH) CORN TORTILLAS, EITHER FRESH OR WARMED*

1 CLOVE GARLIC, PEELED

10 TEASPOONS BUTTER

1 TABLESPOON CILANTRO, MINCED (OPTIONAL)

In a medium bowl, gently combine the cheese and crabmeat. Add the bell pepper and green onions. Spread 2 tablespoons of the mixture over half of each warmed corn tortilla, and fold over the other half to cover the mixture. Repeat with all tortillas and the remaining filling. Cover with plastic wrap to keep fresh. When ready to grill, place the peeled garlic clove securely on the end of a fork, and in a large skillet or on a griddle, melt 1 teaspoon of butter and rub the surface with the garlic. Grill the stuffed quesadillas, turning gently until golden and crispy on each side. Grill each quesadilla approximately 3 to 6 minutes. Repeat for remaining quesadillas.

*If tortillas are not fresh, warm them in a microwave by placing 3 or 4 tortillas at a time in a small plastic bag and heating them at 50% power for 45 to 60 seconds. This will make them more pliable to work with.

Roasted Garlic Chicken Quesadilla

This is my rendition of an oven-fired pizza. Using a prepared Alfredo sauce is an effortless way to add an array of flavors without adding a lot of other ingredients. (Makes 4 to 6 servings)

2 BONELESS CHICKEN BREAST HALVES,
4 TO 6 OUNCES EACH

6 CLOVES GARLIC, PEELED

2 TABLESPOONS OLIVE OIL

3 (10- TO 12-INCH) FLOUR TORTILLAS

6 TABLESPOONS PREPARED ALFREDO SAUCE

1½ CUPS MUSHROOMS, SLICED

¼ CUP RED ONION, THINLY SLICED

½ POUND MONTEREY JACK CHEESE, SHREDDED

Preheat oven to 350°F. To roast the chicken and garlic, wash and dry the chicken pieces, and rub them with 1 tablespoon of the oil. Seal the pieces tightly together in foil. Peel the garlic, place the whole cloves on a separate piece of foil, drizzle with remaining oil, and seal tightly. Place both foil packets in a baking dish, and bake for 20 minutes. Let the chicken and garlic cool a bit, and then thinly slice the garlic and shred or chop the chicken into bite-sized pieces, and set aside.

Brush each tortilla with 2 tablespoons of the Alfredo sauce. Place one-third of the mushrooms, red onion, and chicken on top of each of the tortillas. Sprinkle one-third of the cheese over each tortilla, and top each with one-third of the garlic slices. Place each quesadilla on a baking sheet and broil for 8 to 10 minutes until the cheese is bubbly and the edges of the tortilla are brown. Slice into wedges and serve.

Garden Quesadilla

◎

A little fresh spinach, onion, and garlic, all sautéed in butter, fill my kitchen with an aroma that I love. In my home, Garden Quesadillas aren't just appetizers, they're also a full meal. (Makes 10 slices or 4 servings)

3 TABLESPOONS UNSALTED BUTTER
½ POUND FRESH SPINACH, CLEANED, DRIED, AND CHOPPED*
1 SMALL WHITE ONION, FINELY CHOPPED
2 CLOVES GARLIC, MINCED
1 TABLESPOON CRUSHED RED PEPPER FLAKES
PINCH OF SALT
1 POUND MONTEREY JACK OR ASADERO CHEESE, GRATED
5 MEDIUM-SIZED FLOUR TORTILLAS
FIESTA TACO SALSA (PAGE 12)

Melt 2 tablespoons of the butter in a medium skillet and sauté the spinach, onion, and garlic until the onions are almost translucent. Let cool, and then season with crushed red pepper and salt. Fold the grated cheese into the spinach mixture, and spread 2 to 3 tablespoons of the mixture onto half of each tortilla. Fold the tortilla in half to cover the mixture.

In a skillet or on a heavy griddle, melt about ½ teaspoon of the remaining butter for each filled tortilla, and grill the tortillas one at a time on each side until golden brown. Cut each tortilla in half, place on a serving plate, and serve with Fiesta Taco Salsa.

*If you'd like, substitute a 10-ounce package of frozen spinach, chopped and drained.

Pesto Cilantro Quesadilla

◎

This zesty cheese crisp, with lots of herbs, cheeses, and fresh vine-ripened tomato slices has an outrageous taste that everyone will love. It is a perfect example of infused cooking—a taste of Italian mixed with a bit of fresh-Mex. (Makes 4 to 6 servings)

3 TABLESPOONS PREPARED PESTO SAUCE
4 TEASPOONS CILANTRO, MINCED
½ POUND MONTEREY JACK CHEESE, GRATED
4 (10- TO 12-INCH) FLOUR TORTILLAS
3 TO 4 MEDIUM VINE-RIPENED TOMATOES, THINLY SLICED
PARMESAN CHEESE, GRATED

Evenly divide the pesto sauce, minced cilantro, and Monterey Jack cheese on each tortilla. Broil each quesadilla until the edges are brown and crispy and the cheese is bubbly. Remove from the flame, and divide the tomato slices among the warm quesadillas. Sprinkle with Parmesan cheese. Cut each quesadilla into 6 slices and serve.

Twilight Gatherings

Twilight gatherings with good friends and good food are at the heart of *Fiesta* entertaining. As the host, you have the opportunity to create an atmosphere of fun by turning simple meals into culinary delights. I have included an appetizing array of soups and entrées that will turn casual eating into a full dining experience. The steam that rises from a *Mexicali* sopa can be irresistible. Add Sonora Chicken Tacos and Shrimp Avocado Nachos and you've got a meal that will satisfy everyone. Kettle favorites such as Sopa de Lima or a big pot of frijoles are popular in many regions of Mexico, while Grilled Carne Asada Tortas with Caramelized Onions or Chile-Rubbed Shrimp with Cilantro Butter are grilled favorites with a contemporary West Coast twist. Accents of earthy chipotle chile and honey drizzled over delicate chicken skewers, fresh fish wrapped in warm tortillas, and tangy chile pasta with fresh produce bring together the essence of California cooking and traditional Mexican fare.

FIREBREATHING GLAZED CHIPOTLE
CHICKEN SKEWERS
MARGARITA CHICKEN
CARNE ASADA CLASSICO
POLLO ASADA
GRILLED CARNE ASADA TORTAS WITH
CARAMELIZED ONIONS
GRILLED TUNA STEAK TACOS
BAJA TACOS WITH
CHIPOTLE RANCH DRESSING
SONORA CHICKEN TACOS
MACHACA MINI-CHIMICHANGAS
GLORIOUS CHICKEN NACHOS
SHRIMP AVOCADO NACHOS
SIRLOIN NACHOS GRANDE WITH
CHIPOTLE CHILE LIME SAUCE
CHILE-RUBBED SHRIMP WITH
CILANTRO BUTTER
GREEN CHILE CHICKEN ALFREDO
CLASSIC CARNITAS
RED CHILE CARNITAS
BAKED POTATO SOPA Y CHILE
CALDO DE POLLO
SOPA DE LIMA
SALPICON
SPICY SUN BOWL CHOWDER
INCREDIBLE GREEN CHILE STEW
POT OF FRIJOLES

Firebreathing Glazed Chipotle Chicken Skewers

These grilled chicken skewers with fiery smoky chipotle chile sauce will spice up your life and knock you off your feet! If you find the need to tame the heat, add your favorite barbecue sauce. This will complement the smoky, rich flavor of the chipotle sauce.

(Makes 6 servings)

1 CAN (7 OUNCES) CHIPOTLE CHILES
IN ADOBO SAUCE*

¼ CUP HONEY

2 TABLESPOONS OLIVE OIL

6 BONELESS CHICKEN BREAST
HALVES, 4 TO 6 OUNCES EACH,
CUT INTO 1½ INCH CUBES

Soak 6 8-inch wooden skewers in water for about 2 hours to prevent them from catching fire during grilling. Carefully seed the chipotle chiles. Puree the chiles and adobo sauce in a blender until smooth. Place the honey and olive oil in a medium bowl. Thread 6 cubes of chicken on each skewer.

Grill over medium heat for 3 to 5 minutes, and then turn and grill on the other side for 3 to 5 minutes until the juices run clear. Reduce heat or move the skewers to the outer edge of the grill. Brush each skewer with the glaze and grill 2 to 3 more minutes, turning slowly until the chicken is slightly charred.

*For a milder, smoother sauce, halve the amount of chipotle chile in adobo sauce and add ½ cup of your favorite barbecue sauce.

Margarita Chicken

🌵

I developed this recipe while doing a feature on olive oils for my television show on KTSM/NBC in El Paso. Olive oil seals in the juices while grilling. It has become a favorite with my viewers; they love the tangy margarita flavor. (Makes 6 servings)

¼ CUP FRESH LIME JUICE, SQUEEZED FROM 3 TO 4 LIMES

2 TABLESPOONS OLIVE OIL

2 CLOVES GARLIC, PEELED AND MINCED

2 TABLESPOONS TEQUILA

2 TABLESPOONS ORANGE-FLAVORED LIQUEUR, SUCH AS TRIPLE SEC, COINTREAU, OR GRAND MARNIER

1 TABLESPOON FRESH CILANTRO, CHOPPED

6 MEDIUM-SIZED SKINLESS, BONELESS CHICKEN BREAST HALVES

1 ORANGE, SLICED

1 LIME, SLICED

2 TABLESPOONS HONEY

Combine the lime juice, oil, garlic, tequila, liqueur, and cilantro in a small bowl. Pierce the chicken with a fork and place the pieces in a large resealable plastic bag, along with half of the orange and lime slices. Pour all but 2 tablespoons of the marinade over the chicken, close the bag, and refrigerate for 3 to 4 hours, occasionally using your hands outside the bag to work the marinade into the chicken.

Grill the chicken over a medium fire for 6 to 8 minutes on each side, until the chicken is opaque and the juices run clear. Combine the remaining 2 tablespoons of marinade with the honey. After you remove the chicken from the grill, brush it with the honey glaze, garnish with remaining orange and lime slices, and serve.

Carne Asada Classico

Spicy, marinated meats sizzling on the grill—
that is a Mexican-style barbecue. When I was
growing up in southern Arizona, Carne Asada
(pronounced "car-neh ah-sah-dah") was a
mainstay for any weekend gathering and was
readily available at a local market. While I was
away at college, I discovered I couldn't find
carne in any grocery store or local meat market,
so I created this recipe. It can be used with
skirt steak and flank steak, or even on chicken.
So grab a warm tortilla, a little grilled *carne*, and
pile it high with fresh salsa and diced avocado.
(Makes 4 to 6 servings)

6 MEDIUM-SIZED LEMONS

2 TABLESPOONS RED BELL PEPPER, MINCED

3 CLOVES GARLIC, MINCED

1 CAN (7 OUNCES) PICKLED JALAPEÑO CHILES,

SLICED IN THEIR OWN JUICE*

1 BOTTLE (10 OUNCES) TERIYAKI SAUCE

1 TABLESPOON SUGAR

2 TEASPOONS SALT

3 POUNDS FLANK STEAK OR SKIRT STEAK,

RINSED AND PATTED DRY

12 FRESH FLOUR TORTILLAS,

8 TO 10 INCHES IN DIAMETER, WARMED

2 OR 3 RIPE AVOCADOS,

PEELED AND DICED JUST BEFORE SERVING

PICO DE GALLO (PAGE 10)

In a medium glass bowl, combine the juice of
five of the lemons with the minced bell pepper,
garlic, jalapeños, teriyaki sauce, sugar, and salt.
Mix until the sugar and salt have dissolved.
Place the meat in a large sealable plastic bag
and pour the marinade into the bag with the
meat. Slice the remaining lemon into thin
rounds and place them in the bag. Seal the bag
and work the marinade through the meat with
your hands. Refrigerate for at least 2 to 3 hours
and up to 24 hours, occasionally working the
marinade around from the outside of the bag
with your hands.

Grill the meat over a medium fire for 6 to 8
minutes on each side. The meat should be
just barely pink inside. Remove from the
grill, and slice the meat into long, thin strips
about one-half inch thick. Wrap the meat in
warm tortillas. (The tortillas, by the way,
should be fresh. Call your grocer to find out
the days when fresh tortillas arrive.) Garnish
with fresh avocado and Pico de Gallo.

*If you cannot find pickled jalapeños in the can, use ¾
cup of pickled (sliced) jalapeño in the jar, usually found in
the pickle and olive section of your market. Also, when I
am rushed, I will substitute one packet of dry Italian salad
dressing mix for the bell pepper, garlic, sugar, and salt. It
gives all the seasonings without the measuring and chopping.

Pollo Asada

This is a tasty and lighter version of Carne Asada and a flavorful way to marinate chicken breasts. For large gatherings I like to serve both Carne (meat, usually beef) and Pollo (chicken) Asada, giving my guests a tasty variety to enjoy. (Makes 4 to 6 servings)

6 MEDIUM-SIZED LEMONS

2 TABLESPOONS RED BELL PEPPER, MINCED

3 CLOVES GARLIC, MINCED

1 CAN (7 OUNCES) PICKLED JALAPEÑO CHILES, SLICED IN THEIR OWN JUICE*

1 BOTTLE (10 OUNCES) TERIYAKI SAUCE

1 TABLESPOON SUGAR

2 TEASPOONS SALT

6 SKINLESS CHICKEN-BREAST HALVES, 4 TO 6 OUNCES EACH

12 FRESH FLOUR TORTILLAS, 8 TO 10 INCHES IN DIAMETER, WARMED

In a medium glass bowl, combine the juice of five of the lemons with the minced bell pepper, garlic, jalapeños, teriyaki sauce, sugar, and salt. Mix until the sugar and salt have dissolved. Place the chicken in a large resealable plastic bag and pour the marinade into the bag with the meat. Slice the remaining lemon into thin rounds and place them in the bag. Seal the bag and work the marinade through the chicken with your hands. Refrigerate for 1 to 2 hours up to 24 hours in advance, occasionally working the marinade around from the outside of the bag with your hands.

Grill the chicken for about 5 minutes on each side over a medium-low fire, or until the juices run clear when you cut into the center. Slice the chicken into long, thin strips about one-half inch thick, and wrap the chicken in warm tortillas (the tortillas should be fresh). Garnish with any of the following: Fiesta Taco Salsa (page 12), Pico de Gallo (page 10), Fiesta Verde Sauce (page 14), or Avocado Tossa (page 15).

*If you cannot find pickled jalapeños in the can, use ¾ cup of pickled (sliced) jalapeño in the jar, usually found in the pickle and olive section of your market. Also, when I am rushed, I will substitute one packet of dry Italian salad dressing mix for the bell pepper, garlic, sugar, and salt. It gives all the seasonings without the measuring and chopping.

Grilled Carne Asada Tortas with Caramelized Onions

🌵

These small, overstuffed Mexican sandwiches are served on bolillos (boh-LEE-yohs), crusty, hollowed-out rolls. If you have a hard time finding bolillos, try small, crisp French rolls or sourdough rolls. These warm bundles are delicious. (Makes 6 Servings)

CARNE ASADA CLASSICO (PAGE 51)

2 TABLESPOONS BUTTER

3 TABLESPOONS OLIVE OIL

2 TABLESPOONS SUGAR

6 ONIONS, PEELED AND SLICED INTO ½-INCH RINGS

6 BOLILLO BUNS OR FRENCH ROLLS

3 AVOCADOS, PEELED, PITTED, AND SLICED

KOSHER SALT TO TASTE

CRACKED BLACK PEPPER TO TASTE

Grill meat as directed in the Carne Asada Classico recipe. While the meat is grilling, melt the butter and 2 tablespoons of the olive oil over medium heat in a large saucepan. Add the sugar, and stir until dissolved. Add the onions, cover, and cook until the onions soften, 4 to 6 minutes. Remove the lid, and continue cooking over medium-low heat until the onions begin to caramelize, about 10 to 12 minutes. Remove when the onions are evenly browned.

Slice the buns lengthwise with a serrated knife, and brush the insides with the remaining olive oil. Place on the grill, oiled side down, for 2 to 3 minutes until grill marks appear on the bread. Divide the meat among the six bottom halves of the buns. Top the meat with onions and avocado slices, and then season with salt and pepper. Garnish with Pico de Gallo (page 10) or Fresh Salsa Verde (page 13).

Grilled Tuna Steak Tacos

🌵

This taco brings together some intricate flavors. The result is so unusual that you'll crave another and then another. The spicy tropical salsa gives a contemporary accent to the light, delicate fish, and it's all wrapped in a fresh corn tortilla. Fiery Citrus Salsa adds the crowning glory to these tropical tacos. (Makes 8 servings)

2 TUNA STEAKS, CUT 1-INCH THICK,
SPRINKLED WITH GARLIC SALT AND BRUSHED WITH OLIVE OIL
8 FRESH CORN TORTILLAS, 6 INCHES IN DIAMETER
½ CUP PREPARED RANCH SALAD DRESSING
2 CUPS CABBAGE OR ICEBERG LETTUCE, SHREDDED
FIERY CITRUS SALSA (PAGE 15)

Brush your grill rack with vegetable oil to prevent the tuna from sticking. Grill the steaks over medium heat for 6 to 8 minutes on each side. Remove from heat, let stand for 5 minutes, and cut into bite-sized chunks. Fold 5 to 6 chunks of the tuna into each of the warmed tortillas. Garnish each tuna tortilla with a portion of ranch dressing, chilled Fiery Citrus Salsa, and the shredded cabbage or lettuce. Warm the tortillas over the grill before serving.

Baja Tacos with Chipotle Ranch Dressing

This Southern California favorite is catching on all over the country. In this delicious recipe, fresh fish is lightly battered and folded into a warm corn tortilla. The creamy chipotle dressing makes these tacos come alive. (Makes 6 servings)

1 CUP ALL-PURPOSE FLOUR

½ TEASPOON KOSHER SALT

½ TEASPOON CRACKED PEPPER

1½ POUNDS FRESH SEA BASS, HALIBUT, SWORDFISH,
OR COD, CUT INTO 1-INCH CHUNKS

VEGETABLE OIL

12 TO 14 FRESH CORN TORTILLAS, 6 INCHES IN DIAMETER, WARMED

1 CUP SHREDDED GREEN CABBAGE

1 CUP SHREDDED RED CABBAGE

1 MEDIUM WHITE ONION, MINCED

PICO DE GALLO (PAGE 10)

To cook the fish, combine the flour, salt, and pepper in a shallow bowl, and dredge the fish chunks in this mixture. Line a platter with paper towels. Place 2 to 3 inches of oil in a large skillet, and heat the oil until the temperature measures 350°F on a candy thermometer. Drop 4 or 5 chunks of the dredged fish into the hot oil, and deep-fry for 2 to 3 minutes, until the fish chunks are golden brown. Remove the fish from the oil and place on platter. Fold into one of the warmed tortillas. Repeat with remaining fish and tortillas. Garnish each with a portion of the chipotle ranch dressing, and then with a little cabbage and onion. Top with a bit of the Pico de Gallo.

Chipotle Ranch Dressing

¾ CUP PREPARED RANCH DRESSING

¼ CUP SOUR CREAM

1 TEASPOON CHIPOTLE CHILE IN ADOBO SAUCE, SEEDED AND MINCED

To make the dressing, thoroughly blend together the prepared ranch dressing and the sour cream, add the minced chile, and refrigerate until ready to serve.

Sonora Chicken Tacos

The state of Sonora was Mexico's wheat country, so many recipes from that region use flour tortillas instead of corn tortillas. These tasty party tacos are full of a flavorful shredded chicken that has been poached in a strong broth, and then wrapped in a light, crispy flour tortilla.
(Makes 42 mini-tacos)

1 WHOLE CHICKEN, 3 TO 4 POUNDS

3 TABLESPOONS GRANULATED CHICKEN BOUILLON

2 GREEN ONIONS, MINCED

KOSHER SALT TO TASTE

6 TO 8 FLOUR TORTILLAS, EACH 8 INCHES IN DIAMETER AND CUT INTO 6 WEDGES

VEGETABLE OIL

FIESTA TACO SALSA (PAGE 12)

Place the chicken in a large pot and cover with water. Add the bouillon. Cook, covered, over medium-high heat for approximately 45 minutes, until the meat pulls away easily from the bone. Let the chicken cool in its own stock for 15 to 20 minutes. Place the chicken on a cutting board and pull the meat away, discarding bones, fat, and skin. Shred the chicken, and let cool. Add the green onions and salt to the cooled chicken.

Place a heaping tablespoon of the shredded chicken on the widest end of each tortilla wedge. Roll up and secure the center of each little taco with a toothpick. Place in a large plastic bag to keep fresh. Repeat with the remaining chicken and tortillas.

Pour 2 to 3 inches of oil into a large, deep skillet. Heat oil over medium-high heat until the temperature reads 350°F on a candy thermometer, and carefully deep-fry the chicken tacos for 2 to 3 minutes, until they are golden brown. Be careful—the chicken can pop and hot oil can spray during frying. Serve warm or at room temperature with Fiesta Taco Salsa.

Machaca Mini-Chimichangas

Years ago, there was no refrigeration in the desert areas of Sonora, Mexico, so beef was often served machaca-style, preserved through salting and dehydrating. It was known more as a "jerky," and it was used in burritos and main dishes. Through the years, it has evolved into a tender, shredded meat dish full of spices and served any time during the day. Today, I serve it as an entrée accompanied by a fresh flour tortilla or as a filling in these little crispy chimichangas. I have found that baking instead of frying these little burritos saves calories and time. (Makes 8 to 10 servings)

1 CHUCK ROAST, 2 TO 3 POUNDS

1 MEDIUM YELLOW ONION, QUARTERED

6 WHOLE CLOVES GARLIC

1 TABLESPOON PLUS 2 TEASPOONS KOSHER SALT

2 TABLESPOONS VEGETABLE OIL

1 VINE-RIPENED TOMATO, SEEDED AND CHOPPED

1 MEDIUM YELLOW ONION, CHOPPED

1 CUP GREEN CHILE, ROASTED,

PEELED, AND CHOPPED

16 FLOUR TORTILLAS, EACH 8 INCHES IN DIAMETER

1 TO 2 CUPS VEGETABLE OIL (OPTIONAL)

Place the roast in a heavy pot with enough water to cover. Add the quartered onion, garlic, and 1 tablespoon of the salt. Cover, bring to a low boil, and cook over medium-high heat for 3 to 4 hours, until the meat pulls away easily. Remove the meat, let cool slightly, and shred, discarding any fat.

Pour the 2 tablespoons of vegetable oil into a large skillet, and sauté the tomato, onion, and green chile over medium heat. When the vegetables have softened, add the shredded meat, season with the remaining 2 teaspoons of salt, cover the skillet, and cook, stirring occasionally, until heated through, about 15 minutes.

Place 2 heaping tablespoons of the beef filling on a tortilla, and using your fingers, shape the filling into a small rectangle in the center of the tortilla. Fold the sides of the tortilla up around the short ends of the rectangle, and then roll the rest of the tortilla and secure it with toothpicks an inch from

each end. Place each burrito in a large plastic bag, or wrap it in plastic wrap and refrigerate to keep the burritos firm and shaped properly.

Remove the burritos from the refrigerator and let stand at room temperature in the plastic bag for 15 minutes. Brush each burrito with a light coating of vegetable oil and place on a baking sheet, seam-side down, 2 inches apart. Bake for 20 minutes at 350°F until golden brown and crispy. Turn each chimichanga over, and bake for 10 more minutes until golden brown and crispy all over. Carefully slice in half at an angle (for more of a decorative look) between the toothpicks, and serve.

Glorious Chicken Nachos

The basic nachos—crispy corn tortillas layered with melted cheddar cheese and topped with spicy pickled jalapeño slices—were at one time, the essence of the Mexican appetizer. Today, they have become a meal in themselves. We often have "Nacho Night" at my house, serving a platter of these wonderful *antojitos* as the main dish. I like to layer the traditional nacho with unexpected ingredients and combinations. In this one, the combination of Monterey Jack cheese and caramelized onions adds character, and the green chile in place of the traditional jalapeño gives a smoother chile accent. (Makes 6 to 8 servings)

4 CLOVES GARLIC, MINCED

3 TABLESPOONS OLIVE OIL

2 CHICKEN BREAST HALVES, CUT INTO 2-INCH CHUNKS

1 TEASPOON SUGAR

PINCH OF KOSHER SALT

2 MEDIUM YELLOW ONIONS, PEELED AND
SLICED INTO ½-INCH RINGS

24 TORTILLA CHIPS

¾ POUND MONTEREY JACK CHEESE, GRATED

½ CUP GREEN CHILE, CHOPPED

Sauté the garlic in 2 tablespoons of the oil in a large skillet over medium-high heat for 2 to 3 minutes, until softened. Add the chicken, and cook over medium-high heat until the pan juices have been absorbed and the chicken is lightly browned and slightly crispy, about 15 minutes. Place the chicken on a cutting board, cut into bite-sized pieces, and set aside.

Add the remaining 1 tablespoon of oil, sugar, and salt to the skillet, blend, and add the onion rings. Cook, stirring often, over medium heat until the onions cook down and caramelize, about 15 minutes. Place the onions on a cutting board and cut into ½-inch pieces.

Place the chips on a large ovenproof platter. Sprinkle them with ½ pound of the grated cheese, the chicken, and the caramelized onions. Top with the remaining cheese and green chile. Bake in a preheated oven at 350°F for 12 to 15 minutes, until the cheese is completely melted.

Shrimp Avocado Nachos

I like to serve these fresh, mouth-watering nachos just at the onset of summer, a season full of relaxing warm nights with good food and good conversation. The shrimp salsa is a tangy relish that crowns this creamy nacho platter, infusing coastal flavors with Mexican tradition.
(Makes 36 nachos)

1 POUND MEDIUM SHRIMP

1 TABLESPOON FRESH CILANTRO, MINCED

1 FRESH JALAPEÑO CHILE, SEEDED AND DICED

⅓ CUP RED ONION, MINCED

2 MEDIUM AVOCADOS, RIPE BUT FIRM

JUICE OF 2 LIMES

½ POUND MONTEREY JACK CHEESE, GRATED

36 CORN TORTILLA CHIPS

To cook the shrimp, fill a large pot ¾ full with water and bring to a boil. Carefully add the shrimp to the boiling water and cook 3 to 4 minutes until the shrimp turn pinkish orange. Remove shrimp with a slotted spoon, let them cool, and then shell, devein, place in a colander, rinse with cool water, let drain, and refrigerate for 1 hour. Coarsely chop the shrimp and toss in a large bowl with cilantro, jalapeño, and onion. Just before serving, peel, seed, and dice the avocados into bite-sized chunks. Add the lime juice and avocado to the salsa mixture, and toss gently.

Place the chips side by side on an ovenproof platter. Sprinkle the grated cheese over the chips, and broil until the cheese is melted and bubbly, about 6 to 8 minutes. Remove from the oven, top immediately with the shrimp salsa, and serve.

Sirloin Nachos Grande with Chipotle Chile Lime Sauce

Layers of refried beans and melted cheese set the foundation for these nachos. The sirloin, cooked fajita-style, adds a sizzling texture to this dish. I add a *Mexicali*-style dipping sauce for a cool, creamy accent of flavors.
(Makes 4 to 6 servings)

1½ CUPS REFRIED BEANS*

2 CLOVES GARLIC, PEELED AND MINCED

2 TABLESPOONS OLIVE OIL

6 OUNCES SIRLOIN STEAK, SLICED INTO THIN STRIPS

JUICE OF ½ LEMON

15 TO 20 ROUND CORN TORTILLA CHIPS

¼ POUND CHEDDAR CHEESE, GRATED

¼ POUND MONTEREY JACK CHEESE, GRATED

2 TABLESPOONS RED BELL PEPPER, CHOPPED

1 GREEN ONION, CHOPPED

CHIPOTLE CHILE LIME SAUCE (SEE RECIPE BELOW)

Spread the beans on the bottom of a medium-sized, ovenproof serving platter or pie plate and keep warm in a preheated 200°F oven. Meanwhile, sauté the garlic in the olive oil in a large skillet over medium heat. As the garlic softens, increase heat to high, add the sirloin and the lemon juice, grill, and toss until the juice has evaporated and the meat starts to char. Remove from heat. Remove the warm beans from the oven, turn the oven to broil, and cover the beans with tortilla chips. Layer the chips with cheddar cheese, sirloin, and Monterey Jack cheese. Broil the nachos until the cheese has melted and is bubbling, about 10 to 12 minutes. Remove and garnish with red bell pepper and green onion. Serve immediately with Chipotle Chile Lime Sauce on the side for dipping.

*There are high-quality canned refried beans in your Mexican food section at the market.

Chipotle Chile Lime Sauce

8 OUNCES SOUR CREAM

2 TO 3 CHIPOTLE CHILES IN ADOBO SAUCE, SEEDED AND MINCED

JUICE OF ½ LIME

Thoroughly combine all ingredients and chill until ready to serve.

Chile-Rubbed Shrimp with Cilantro Butter

❦

This recipe has only a few spices and only a few steps. I love it because it's sophisticated, stress-free, and simply delicious. This light and healthy dish is the true essence of Mexican coastal cuisine. Fresh cilantro plus the sweetness of unsalted butter adds a new dimension to the dipping sauce. Crack open a couple of beers, and you'll feel like you're on a Mexican beach. (Makes 4 servings)

16 JUMBO SHRIMP, DEVEINED AND PEELED, TAILS INTACT

2 TABLESPOONS OLIVE OIL

2 TABLESPOONS CRUSHED RED PEPPER FLAKES

1 TABLESPOON KOSHER SALT

¼ POUND (1 STICK) UNSALTED BUTTER

1 TABLESPOON FRESH CILANTRO, FINELY CHOPPED

You'll need 4 skewers. If they're wooden, soak them in water for 1-2 hours. Thread 4 shrimp on each skewer, and brush the shrimp with olive oil. Sprinkle the shrimp with the crushed red pepper and salt. You can either grill or broil the shrimp. Grill over a medium-low fire for 2 to 4 minutes, turning once, until the shrimp turn pinkish orange and no juices flow, or broil in a preheated oven for a few minutes on each side, until the shrimp turn a bright, pinkish orange. While the shrimp are grilling, melt the butter and cilantro in a small saucepan over low heat on the stovetop. Simmer and stir for 2 to 3 minutes to thoroughly blend the flavors. Remove the shrimp from the skewers, and serve with the warm Cilantro Butter as a dipping sauce.

Green Chile Chicken Alfredo

This is another of my viewers' favorites. Using a prepared Alfredo sauce shortens the prep time and the ingredient list on this entrée. It is an elegant, infused chile dish that is perfect for company.

(Makes 4 servings)

2 BONELESS CHICKEN BREAST HALVES, CUBED

¼ CUP OLIVE OIL

2 CLOVES GARLIC, MINCED

½ CUP FRESH GREEN CHILE, ROASTED AND CHOPPED

1 CONTAINER (10 OUNCES) PREPARED ALFREDO SAUCE

10 OUNCES SPINACH PASTA, COOKED AL DENTE

2 JALAPEÑOS, SEEDED AND CHOPPED (OPTIONAL)

Brown the chicken in half the olive oil in a large skillet, allowing all of the juices to cook out. Transfer the cooked chicken to a plate and keep warm. Add the remaining 2 tablespoons of olive oil to the skillet and sauté the garlic and green chile over medium heat until the garlic is soft. Reduce to medium-low heat. Add the Alfredo sauce and mix well. Add the cooked chicken and heat through. Serve over hot pasta.

Classic Carnitas

A carnita is a shredded pork taco. Tacos make great party food and these carnitas are no exception. You can casually help yourself, and they are fun to assemble, which makes you come back for more and more. The classic carnita is cooked in lard, but I do it differently. My recipe ties together the distinctive flavors of Mexico with a lighter and healthier preparation. Select a roast with the most marbling; the fat is rendered during roasting, making the carnitas moist and crisp.
(Makes 6 to 8 servings)

1 PORK ROAST, SHOULDER OR BUTT, 4 TO 5 POUNDS

1 MEDIUM YELLOW ONION, SLICED

4 CLOVES GARLIC, WHOLE

3 TABLESPOONS KOSHER SALT

2 TABLESPOONS OLIVE OIL

FRESHLY GROUND PEPPER

2 MEDIUM YELLOW ONIONS, MINCED

4 SERRANO CHILES, SEEDED AND CHOPPED

1 CUP WHOLE MILK

24 FRESH CORN TORTILLAS, 6 INCHES IN DIAMETER

3 LIMES, SLICED INTO THIN WEDGES

FRESH SALSA VERDE (PAGE 13) OR

MANZANA SALSA (PAGE 11)

Place the meat in a large pot with enough water to cover. Add the onion, garlic, and 2 tablespoons of the salt. Bring to a boil. Cook at a low boil over medium heat for 3 to 4 hours, until the meat pulls apart easily. Remove meat from the pot, reserving 1½ cups of the cooking liquid. Let the meat cool slightly, and shred it. If some of the meat does not shred with the grain, chop it into small pieces.

In another large pot, sauté the minced onion and the chopped chile in the olive oil, and season with the remaining salt and pepper. When the onion is soft, about 3 to 4 minutes, add the meat and the 1½ cups of broth. Cook and stir over medium-high heat until the juices have been absorbed, about 15 minutes. Preheat oven to 350°F. Spread the shredded meat evenly in a 13 x 9-inch baking pan, and slowly pour the milk over the meat. Bake for 45 minutes, stirring every 10 to 15 minutes as the meat browns.

Allow your guests to help themselves by spooning meat into fresh corn tortillas. Garnish with lime wedges and Fresh Salsa Verde.

Red Chile Carnitas

You can find classic carnitas, as in the preceding recipe, all along the Mexican border, but Red Chile Carnitas are another story. The Southwest prides itself on its incredible red chile. Try my simplified version of this rich, earthy red chile wrapped around tender pork with a layer of lemon-marinated onions. (Makes 4 to 6 servings)

3 TO 4 MEDIUM RED ONIONS, THINLY SLICED
JUICE OF 4 LEMONS
1 PORK ROAST, SHOULDER OR BUTT, 4 TO 5 POUNDS
4 WHOLE CLOVES GARLIC
2½ TEASPOONS KOSHER SALT
4 CLOVES GARLIC, MINCED
3 CUPS RED CHILE SAUCE* OR PUREE
36 FRESH CORN TORTILLAS, WARMED
2 CUPS GREEN CABBAGE, SHREDDED

Combine the onion slices and lemon juice in a glass bowl, cover, and refrigerate for 2 hours. Place the pork roast, whole garlic cloves, and 1 teaspoon of the salt in a large pot, fill it with enough water to cover the pork, and bring to a boil. Cover and cook for 3 to 4 hours, until the meat is tender and pulls apart easily. Remove meat, allow to cool for 30 minutes, and reserve 1 cup of the liquid. Shred the meat on a cutting board.

In the same pot or skillet sauté the minced garlic in the reserved cooking liquid over medium heat. When the garlic softens, about 2 to 3 minutes, add the remaining salt and the red chile sauce. Stir until blended. Fold in the meat, and mix well so that the meat is coated. Cook, uncovered, over medium-low heat for 30 minutes, stirring occasionally.

Serve with warmed corn tortillas. Place 2 tablespoons of the meat mixture in a tortilla, and garnish each with a bit of the refrigerated lemon-onion and the shredded cabbage.

* Be sure to use fresh, frozen, or canned red chile sauce, not red enchilada sauce, which is much thinner and has less flavor. Both are found in the Mexican food section of your grocery store.

Baked Potato Sopa y Chile

A steamy pot of thick, creamy soup full of russet baked potato chunks and diced green chile is quite inviting any time of year. By baking the potatoes first and leaving the skins on, each chunk creates a rich, earthy flavor. (Makes 4 to 6 servings)

3 MEDIUM BAKING POTATOES

6 SLICES BACON, COOKED CRISP AND CRUMBLED

1 LARGE ONION, CHOPPED

¼ CUP RED BELL PEPPER, CHOPPED

1 QUART WHOLE MILK

2 TEASPOONS SALT

¼ TEASPOON FRESHLY GROUND BLACK PEPPER

1 CUP REGULAR OR LIGHT SOUR CREAM

2 TABLESPOONS FLOUR

12 OUNCES GREEN CHILE, ROASTED, SEEDED, AND CHOPPED

2 GREEN ONIONS, CHOPPED

Bake the potatoes in a preheated 350°F oven for 1½ hours, and allow them to cool slightly. While the potatoes are cooling, cook the bacon, reserving the drippings. Dice the potatoes into bite-sized cubes with the skin left on. Add the diced potatoes, chopped onion, and chopped red pepper to the bacon drippings, cover, and cook over low heat until the vegetables soften, stirring occasionally. Transfer the vegetables to a large pot, and stir in the milk, salt, and black pepper. Bring to a boil over medium-high heat, and then reduce heat to medium.

Combine the sour cream and flour in a medium mixing bowl, and stir to thoroughly blend the ingredients. Slowly add 1 cup of the hot vegetable mixture to the sour cream mixture, and stir until creamy. Then slowly pour the entire sour cream mixture into the hot vegetable mixture to ensure a smooth, creamy chowder. Add the green chile, simmer, and stir over medium heat until the soup bubbles, and serve in individual bowls topped with the crumbled bacon and chopped green onions.

Caldo de Pollo

This simple soup is really a well-garnished broth (caldo) with ingredients that make you feel well nourished and comforted. It is the Mexican version of hearty chicken soup.
(Makes 6 servings)

2 TABLESPOONS BUTTER

1 MEDIUM YELLOW ONION, CHOPPED

2 CLOVES GARLIC, MINCED

4 OUNCES GREEN CHILE, ROASTED,

PEELED, AND MINCED

⅓ CUP TOMATO JUICE

6 CUPS CHICKEN BROTH

2 MEDIUM CHICKEN BREAST HALVES, COOKED AND CUBED

1 TABLESPOON CRUSHED RED PEPPER FLAKES

3 CUPS BROKEN CORN TORTILLA CHIPS

½ POUND MONTEREY JACK CHEESE, GRATED

3 GREEN ONIONS, MINCED

Melt the butter in a large pot and sauté the onion, garlic, and green chile over medium heat until the onions are clear and soft, about 2 to 4 minutes. Add the tomato juice, chicken broth, chicken, and crushed red pepper flakes. Cook over medium-low heat for about 20 minutes. To serve, place ½ cup of the broken tortilla chips in each serving bowl. Ladle the caldo over the chips, and garnish with the cheese and the green onions.

Sopa de Lima

I fell in love with this soup. The delicate citrus flavor of the lime soothes the fiery chile and gives the broth a crisp edge. It's a terrific chicken soup with a tangy twist.
(Makes 6 servings)

1 MEDIUM YELLOW ONION, CHOPPED

2 CLOVES GARLIC, MINCED

4 OUNCES HOT GREEN CHILE,

ROASTED AND MINCED

2 TABLESPOONS OLIVE OIL

2 VINE-RIPENED TOMATOES, SEEDED AND CHOPPED

6 CUPS CHICKEN BROTH

2 MEDIUM CHICKEN BREAST HALVES, COOKED AND CUBED

½ CUP FRESH LIME JUICE (FROM ABOUT 5 LIMES)

1 CUP CRUSHED CORN TORTILLA CHIPS

1-2 AVOCADOS, PEELED, SEEDED, AND CHOPPED

3 GREEN ONIONS, MINCED

3 LIMES, CUT IN WEDGES

Sauté the onion, garlic, and green chile in the olive oil in a skillet over medium heat until the onion is clear and soft, about 2 to 4 minutes. Add the tomatoes, broth, chicken, and lime juice, bring to a boil, reduce to a simmer, and cook uncovered for 10 minutes. Serve in individual bowls and garnish with the tortilla chips, avocado, green onions, and lime wedges.

Salpicon

This is a refreshing meat entrée that is very popular in the El Paso area and through New Mexico. It's a cold marinated beef and cheese salad. I reserve this Mexican delicacy for days when the temperatures inch up beyond 100 degrees. (Makes 6 to 8 servings)

1 BEEF BRISKET, 5 TO 6 POUNDS

3 ONIONS, 2 HALVED, 1 CHOPPED

4 WHOLE CLOVES GARLIC

1 CUP FRESH CILANTRO, CHOPPED

1 CAN (12 OUNCES) WHOLE TOMATOES

1 TEASPOON SALT

1 TEASPOON FRESHLY GROUND BLACK PEPPER

1 CAN (4 OUNCES) CHIPOTLE CHILE, DRAINED AND CHOPPED

¾ CUP PREPARED ITALIAN SALAD DRESSING

1 LARGE TOMATO, CHOPPED

½ POUND MONTEREY JACK CHEESE, CUT INTO ¼-INCH CUBES

2 LARGE AVOCADOS

Place the brisket in a large, heavy pot, cut in half to fit, if necessary, and cover with water. Add halved onions, garlic, and ½ cup of the chopped cilantro, along with the canned tomatoes, salt, and pepper. Cover and cook over medium-high heat at a low boil for 4 hours.

Remove meat and let it cool slightly. Trim away and discard any excess fat, and shred the meat with a fork. Place the shredded beef in a large bowl. Thoroughly combine the chipotle chiles and salad dressing, and pour over the beef. Add the remaining chopped onion, fresh tomato, cilantro, and additional salt and pepper to taste. Toss with the cheese cubes, mixing well, and chill for at least 3 hours. Serve in a decorative bowl garnished with avocado slices.

Spicy Sun Bowl Chowder

I created this chowder for a tailgate segment that my television station was filming for the annual Sun Bowl game, played each December in El Paso. I wanted something quick and spicy for this rowdy football crowd. The weather was chilly, so this creamy chili hit the spot.
(Makes 4 to 6 servings)

2 CANS (10¾ OUNCES EACH) CONDENSED CREAM OF POTATO SOUP

1 CAN (10¾ OUNCES) CONDENSED CREAM OF SHRIMP SOUP

2¼ CUPS HALF-AND-HALF CREAM

1 POUND MEDIUM SHRIMP

½ CUP CORN KERNELS, CANNED OR DEFROSTED, WELL-DRAINED

1 TABLESPOON FRESH CILANTRO, CHOPPED

4 TABLESPOONS (½ STICK) UNSALTED BUTTER

1 TABLESPOON CRUSHED RED PEPPER FLAKES

1 TABLESPOON CHIVES, CHOPPED

To cook the shrimp, fill a large pot ¾ full with water and bring to a boil. Carefully add the shrimp to the boiling water and cook 3 to 4 minutes until the shrimp turn pinkish orange. Remove shrimp with a slotted spoon, let them cool, and then shell, devein, place in a colander, rinse with cool water, let drain, and coarsely chop.

Combine the condensed soups and the half-and-half cream in a large pot over medium heat. Simmer over medium-low heat, stirring occasionally. In a separate skillet, sauté the shrimp, corn, and cilantro in the butter over medium heat for 3 to 4 minutes. Add to the soup mixture and simmer for 10 to 12 minutes. Garnish with the crushed red pepper flakes and chives. If tailgating, transport the soup in an insulated container, and serve in individual foam cups.

Incredible Green Chile Stew

This is a hearty stew that you can eat from a bowl or wrap in fresh flour tortillas and serve as burritos. As you have seen throughout this book, *Mexicali*-style cooking is all about infusing flavors. Here, the garlic, chile, and Mexican tomatoes form a delicious base for the tender meat chunks in a thick stew. (Makes 6 to 8 servings)

2½ TO 3 POUNDS BEEF ROAST OR PORK ROAST

¼ CUP LARD*

1 LARGE ONION, CHOPPED

1 CAN (28 OUNCES) GREEN CHILE, OR

1½ POUNDS FRESH GREEN CHILE, ROASTED AND CHOPPED

2 CANS (14½ OUNCES EACH) MEXICAN-STYLE TOMATOES

4 CLOVES GARLIC, MINCED

KOSHER SALT TO TASTE

1 TABLESPOON COARSELY GROUND BLACK PEPPER

Cut the roast into 1-inch cubes. Brown the meat in a large pot over medium-high heat until the juices are absorbed, about 10 minutes. Melt the lard in a large saucepan over medium heat, add the onion, chile, and tomatoes, and cook until the onion is clear and softened. Combine the green chili tomato mixture with the meat, add the garlic, salt, and pepper, and cook over medium-low heat for 3 to 4 hours. The stew should be thick and hearty.

*I have tried substituting vegetable oil and shortening, but the flavors you get when using a small amount of lard will make all the difference in this dish.

Pot of Frijoles

My mom fixed these beans on cold winter days when we lived in southern Colorado. She would serve large bowls of these frijoles with a warmed flour tortilla or fresh cornbread for an early dinner on those long winter nights. You'll notice that the pork is crisped in lard, which I rarely use. But for this recipe, I've tried many substitutes and nothing tastes as good. (Makes 6 to 8 servings)

3 CUPS (OR 1½ POUNDS) DRIED PINTO BEANS

½ CUP LARD

4 CLOVES GARLIC, MINCED

1 POUND PORK CHUNKS OR THINLY SLICED PIECES, FROM ANY CUT

1 TABLESPOON KOSHER SALT

3 SERRANO CHILES, SEEDED AND CHOPPED

1 MEDIUM ONION, CHOPPED

1½ CUPS GREEN CHILE, ROASTED, PEELED, AND CHOPPED

Thoroughly rinse the beans in a colander and place in a 4- to 6-quart stockpot with enough water to cover by 3 to 4 inches. Bring just to a boil, and then reduce the heat. Partially cover the pot, and watch carefully, adding water as necessary while cooking the beans. Simmer to a low boil, stirring occasionally, for 2½ to 3 hours.

Melt the lard over medium heat in a large skillet. Add the garlic, pork, and 2 teaspoons of the salt. Cook until the pork starts to crisp. Add the serrano chiles and onion. Continue cooking until the vegetables are soft. Remove the pork and vegetables from the skillet with a slotted spoon and set aside. When the beans are ready, add the pork combination to the large pot with the remaining salt and green chile. Simmer for 30 minutes before serving.

Sunset Spirits

No *Mexicali*-style celebration would be complete without the festive taste of a delicious cocktail. Dive into a layered margarita, laced with fresh fruits of the season like raspberries, green apples, and luscious peaches; or try a simple Margarita Martini. Or, for a more specialized taste, try a Dulce de Leche Martini, which is a unique blend of rum, caramel, and cream; or a tall Sangria Spritzer, a combination of raspberry zinfandel spiced with fresh citrus juices. Another crowd-pleaser is the Bloody Mary Bar, which offers an array of tasty accompaniments that are sure to please all your guests. Team any of these interesting cocktails with the flavors of *Mexicali* fare, and before you know it, you'll have a full-blown celebration on your hands.

Through the years, though, I've come to realize that it isn't just the libations and food that make the party. I believe that a host should always set the tone of the party, and to do so, I've included a collection of toasts. Some of the best toasts are straight from the heart, but I've learned from experience that a few good toasts, written down and rehearsed, can have a lasting impact at any social occasion.

MARGARITA CHARDONNAY
MARGARITA MARTINI
FIESTA SALSA MARGARITA
MARGARITA CLASSICO
PINK CADILLAC MARGARITA
FIESTA MARGARITA MIX
FLOATING RASPBERRY MARGARITA
GREEN APPLE SPLASH MARGARITA
PRETTY PEACH MARGARITA
SIMPLY CERVEZAS
TEQUILA GRAND
THE BRAVE BULL
EL MATADOR
BRAVE BULL BLANCO
PIERCED FUZZY NAVEL
PALOMA
CACTUS COLADA
MEXICANA GOLD
WINE WHIMS
DULCE DE LECHE MARTINI
MEXICAN MADRAS MARTINI
MILLENNIUM MARTINI
MELON MARTINI
FIESTA PRIOSKA
FROZEN TUMBLEWEED
CREAMY DREAMY ORANGE FLURRY
SANGRIA SPRITZER
BLOODY MARY BAR
WHITE SANGRIA
SUN-KISSED TEQUILA TEA
SUNSET CHAMPAGNE
LOS TRES AMIGOS!
SUN DEVIL SLAMMER
MEXICAN MUDSLIDE
WOO WOO

Margarita Chardonnay

This is a luscious, frozen cocktail for wine lovers. A blend of lime, orange, and white wine makes the perfect margarita with a lighter hint of alcohol. Serve this frosty white drink in a colorful wine glass or a margarita glass. (Makes 4 servings)

4 OUNCES CHARDONNAY*
6 OUNCES FROZEN LIMEADE CONCENTRATE
1/3 CUP ORANGE JUICE
3 CUPS CRACKED ICE
2 LIMES, CUT INTO QUARTERS
KOSHER SALT
1 ORANGE, THINLY SLICED

Combine the Chardonnay, limeade, and orange juice in a blender, and process for 1 minute. Slowly add the ice and blend to a slushy consistency. Rub the rims of each of 4 margarita glasses with a lime wedge, and then dust each rim with salt and fill each glass with the margarita mixture. Garnish with a twisted orange slice.

*A rich, full-bodied Chardonnay works well with this recipe, or you can also use sauvignon blanc, a crisp, fuller-bodied wine.

I HAVE KNOWN MANY, LIKED A FEW,
LOVED ONE—HERE'S TO YOU!

Margarita Martini

Here's a grand martini *Mexicali*-style. According to many bartenders in Juarez, Mexico, this little drink is actually closer to the original margarita than all the fruity frozen ones we see today. It's tart, refreshing, and potent. (Makes 1 serving)

1 OUNCE TEQUILA
1 OUNCE ORANGE-FLAVORED LIQUEUR,
SUCH AS TRIPLE SEC, COINTREAU,
OR GRAND MARNIER
1 OUNCE FRESH LIME JUICE
CRACKED ICE
1 ORANGE-PEEL TWIST (FOR GARNISH)

Pour the tequila, liqueur, and lime juice into a shaker half filled with cracked ice. Shake well and strain into a martini glass. Garnish with an orange twist.

A BABY WILL MAKE LOVE STRONGER, DAYS SHORTER, NIGHTS LONGER, BANKROLL SMALLER, HOME HAPPIER, CLOTHES SHABBIER, THE PAST FORGOTTEN, AND THE FUTURE WORTH LIVING FOR.

Fiesta Salsa Margarita

Yes, there is such a thing as a vegetarian margarita. Here, the spicy chile blends well with the tequila for an unforgettable experience. (Makes 6 servings)

2 LIMES, CUT INTO WEDGES

KOSHER SALT

1 CUP FIESTA TOMATO RELISH (PAGE 12)

1 CUP SNAPPY TOM COCKTAIL MIX OR

SPICY TOMATO COCKTAIL JUICE

¾ CUP TEQUILA

4 CUPS CRACKED ICE

6 TWISTS OF LIME

Rub the rim of each of six margarita glasses with a lime wedge. Pour the salt on a flat surface, and dip the moistened rim of each glass into the salt. Shake off any excess salt. Combine the Fiesta Tomato Relish, cocktail mix, tequila, and the ice in a blender. Blend for 2 to 3 minutes until slushy. Pour into the salt-rimmed margarita glasses. Garnish with the lime twists.

This is a favorite, but be careful if you've got relatives in the crowd!

THE LORD GIVES US OUR RELATIVES,
THANK GOD WE CAN CHOOSE OUR FRIENDS!

Margarita Classico

This margarita reminds me of the ones served at Chretin's, a legendary Mexican restaurant in Yuma, Arizona. Joe Chretin served these world-famous frosty treats for years. It's the perfect margarita—well balanced, not too tart, and not too sweet. (Makes 4 servings)

1 LIME, CUT INTO WEDGES

KOSHER SALT

6 OUNCES FROZEN LIMEADE CONCENTRATE

¾ CUP TEQUILA

1½ OUNCES ORANGE-FLAVORED LIQUEUR,

SUCH AS TRIPLE SEC, COINTREAU,

OR GRAND MARNIER

¾ CUP LIGHT BEER

5 CUPS CRACKED ICE

Rub the rim of each of 4 margarita glasses with a lime wedge, pour the salt on a flat surface, and dip the moistened rim of each glass into the salt. Shake off any excess salt. Combine the limeade, tequila, liqueur, beer, and ice in a blender. Blend 2 to 3 minutes until slushy. Pour into each glass, and garnish each with a lime wedge.

YOU MAY HAVE A FRIEND,
YOU MAY HAVE A LOVER,
BUT DON'T FORGET,
YOUR BEST FRIEND IS YOUR MOTHER.

Pink Cadillac Margarita

Ahhh, the Pink Cadillac Margarita, my signature drink! This is a great way to serve margaritas to a crowd. The combination of the gold tequila and a hint of grenadine makes a smooth cocktail that your guests will love. I use pre-made margarita mix as the base. This speeds up the preparation time before and during a party. It's a beautiful punch when served in a large, distinctive glass jar or pitcher with cracked ice and sliced lime.
(Makes 4 to 6 servings)

1 BOTTLE (1.75 LITERS) MARGARITA MIX*

12 OUNCES GOLD TEQUILA

⅓ CUP GRENADINE

CRACKED ICE

4 TO 5 LIMES

KOSHER SALT

Combine the margarita mix and the tequila in your serving bowl, and add the grenadine. Cut 2 of the limes into thin slices and add to the mix. Add lots of cracked ice. Cut the remaining limes into wedges. Rub the rims of each of 4 to 6 highball glasses with a lime wedge. Place the salt on a flat surface, and dip the moistened rim of each glass into the salt. Fill each glass with ice, pour some of the margarita mix into each glass, and garnish each drink with a lime wedge.

*There are many good margarita mixes on the market. Use a high-quality mix with a medium sweet-sour balance.

Fiesta Fruit Margaritas

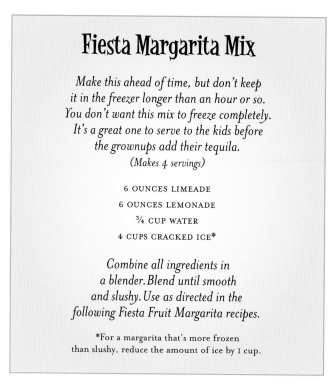

The first time I'd ever seen a margarita was when my parents and their friends took us down to Juarez, just across the border in Mexico. My dad ordered ice-cold Mexican beers for the guys, while my mom and her friends sipped on giant frozen emerald green and azure blue margaritas, served in beautiful glasses. At the age of 10, those fruity frozen marvels looked like the most wonderful snow cones I'd ever seen!

The margarita is a drink with many lives, and it can be as individual as you are. Try layering a margarita with tequila and fruit liqueurs to add a new dimension to this cocktail. I start with the Fiesta Margarita Mix (below), and then match the fresh fruits of the season to fruit-flavored liqueurs.

Fiesta Margarita Mix

Make this ahead of time, but don't keep it in the freezer longer than an hour or so. You don't want this mix to freeze completely. It's a great one to serve to the kids before the grownups add their tequila.

(Makes 4 servings)

6 OUNCES LIMEADE

6 OUNCES LEMONADE

¾ CUP WATER

4 CUPS CRACKED ICE*

Combine all ingredients in a blender. Blend until smooth and slushy. Use as directed in the following Fiesta Fruit Margarita recipes.

*For a margarita that's more frozen than slushy, reduce the amount of ice by 1 cup.

Floating Raspberry Margarita

The rich red berries of summer were the inspiration for this drink. Chambord is often used in martinis, so I just borrowed the raspberry flavor for my margarita. It's a beauty. (Makes 4 servings)

½ CUP TEQUILA

FIESTA MARGARITA MIX

2 OUNCES RASPBERRY-FLAVORED LIQUEUR, SUCH AS CHAMBORD

1 PINT FRESH RASPBERRIES

Pour 1 ounce of the tequila in each of 4 margarita glasses. Divide the Fiesta Margarita Mix among the 4 glasses, and drizzle ½ ounce of the liqueur over each drink. Garnish each drink with 4 fresh raspberries. (I recommend skipping the customary salting of the glass rim for this margarita, as it would take away from the fruity flavor.)

Green Apple Splash Margarita

🌵

I love the flavor and aroma of Sour Green Apple Schnapps. It reminds me of growing up in southern Colorado, where we would wait for the green apples to appear on the trees in our backyard every summer. They were sweet, sour, and we ate so many that we thought we would burst! Try this light and luscious margarita. (Makes 4 servings)

½ CUP TEQUILA
KOSHER SALT
FIESTA MARGARITA MIX (PAGE 80)
2 OUNCES SOUR GREEN APPLE SCHNAPPS
1 GRANNY SMITH APPLE, CUT IN WAFER-THIN WEDGES
JUICE OF ½ LEMON

Moisten the rim of each of 4 margarita glasses with a bit of tequila. Pour the salt on a flat surface, and dip the moistened rim of each glass into the salt. Shake off the excess salt. Pour 1 ounce of the tequila into each glass, along with a portion of the Fiesta Margarita Mix. Drizzle ½ ounce of the Sour Green Apple Schnapps over each drink, and garnish each with a wedge of the apple, brushed with the lemon juice.

WHEN LIFE HANDS YOU LEMONS,
ADD TEQUILA, SOME TRIPLE SEC, A LITTLE SALT,
AND HAVE A MARGARITA.

Pretty Peach Margarita

🌵

The Fiesta Margarita Mix gives a delicate sweet, yet tart flavor to the peach liqueur in this cocktail. The peach liqueur in turn lends a refreshing, smooth flavor to this frosty cocktail. (Makes 4 servings)

4 OUNCES GOLD TEQUILA
KOSHER SALT
FIESTA MARGARITA MIX (PAGE 80)
2 OUNCES PEACH SCHNAPPS
1 RIPE, FIRM PEACH,
PEELED, PITTED, AND CHOPPED

Moisten the rim of each glass with a bit of tequila. Pour the salt on a flat surface, dip the moistened rim of each glass into the salt, and shake off any excess. Pour 1 ounce of the tequila in each margarita glass, and divide the Fiesta Margarita Mix among the 4 glasses. Drizzle an equal amount of Schnapps over each drink, and garnish with a few peach chunks.

I LOVE EVERYTHING OLD—
OLD FRIENDS, OLD TIMES, OLD MANNERS,
OLD BOOKS, AGED TEQUILA, AND OLD WINES.

Simply Cervezas

Frosty margaritas are not the only drink I serve with my *Fiesta Mexicali* fare. It is most definitely a cerveza cuisine as well. A good quality brew quenches your thirst and it cools down the fiery flavors. Grab a large galvanized tub, fill it with ice, and stock it with some beers. It'll be the focal point of the party. I like Mexican beer, as it's authentic, and it goes well with the Mexican food. A twist of lime is a must for Corona, Pacifico, Tecate, or Dos Equis, which are the most commonly imported brews.

Here are a few tips on matching beers and *Fiesta Mexicali* foods:

• Pilsners and pale ales go well with lime- or vinegar-flavored dishes, such as ceviches, salsas, and salads.

• Light lagers and wheat beers go with seafood, chicken, and tomato sauces.

• Blonde ales and medium lagers go well with pork dishes such as carnitas.

• Bock and dark lagers are good matches for Carne Asada and Machaca dishes.

Again, it is a matter of personal taste. Finding a favorite combination can be hard work, but someone's got to do it! *Salud!*

Tequila Grand

I kicked this Tequila Sunrise up a few notches. This tall, cool, thirst-quencher has an intricate balance of flavors, in which each fruit juice complements the others. (Makes 1 serving)

1½ OUNCES TEQUILA

SPLASH OF ORANGE-FLAVORED LIQUEUR,

SUCH AS TRIPLE SEC, COINTREAU, OR GRAND MARNIER

4 OUNCES CRANBERRY JUICE

CRACKED ICE

¼ OUNCE PINEAPPLE JUICE

¼ OUNCE ORANGE JUICE

Pour the tequila, liqueur, and cranberry juice into a collins glass half filled with cracked ice. Stir, and top with pineapple and orange juice.

This traditional Mexican toast is always appropriate for a festive occasion.

SALUD, AMOR, Y PESETAS Y EL TIEMPO PARA GUSTARLOS!

(Health, love, and money and the time to enjoy them.)

The Brave Bull

This drink captures the distinctive flavors of Mexico—gold tequila and coffee-flavored liqueur blended together. Serve as a potent cocktail, or mix with your after-dinner coffee. (Makes 1 serving)

2 OUNCES GOLD TEQUILA

1 OUNCE COFFEE-FLAVORED LIQUEUR,

SUCH AS KAHLUÁ

CRACKED ICE

In a shaker half filled with ice, combine the tequila and the liqueur. Shake well, and strain into a martini glass or a sour-style glass.

El Matador

Cool off with this elegant and refreshing midday libation. The pineapple juice wraps around the tequila with a zesty zing. Serve it poolside or out on the patio. (Makes 1 serving)

1½ OUNCES GOLD TEQUILA

3 OUNCES PINEAPPLE JUICE

JUICE OF ½ LIME

CRACKED ICE

Pour the tequila, pineapple juice, and lime juice into a shaker half filled with cracked ice. Shake well, and strain into a fluted champagne glass.

Brave Bull Blanco

This is a rich cocktail that I like to use as an after-dinner drink. I like to nurse it along for a smooth, relaxing experience. The cream balances the flavors of the liqueur and tequila. (Makes 1 serving)

1½ OUNCES GOLD TEQUILA

1½ OUNCES COFFEE-FLAVORED LIQUEUR,

SUCH AS KAHLÚA

1½ OUNCES HEAVY CREAM

CRACKED ICE

Combine the tequila, liqueur, and cream in a shaker half filled with ice. Shake well, and strain into an Old-Fashioned glass half full of cracked ice.

Pierced Fuzzy Navel

It's the tequila in place of vodka that makes this fuzzy navel fun to drink! The combination of the Schnapps and orange juice gives a nice finish to the tequila. (Makes 1 serving)

1 OUNCE TEQUILA

1½ OUNCES PEACH SCHNAPPS

CRACKED ICE

½ OUNCE FRESH-SQUEEZED ORANGE JUICE, CHILLED

Pour tequila and Schnapps into a shaker with cracked ice. Shake well, and pour into a martini glass. Top with the orange juice.

Paloma

This is a trendy, new drink straight from Guadalajara, Mexico, the tequila capital of the world. Many tequila drinkers in this region regard the margarita as passé, a cocktail for Gringos and tourists. The locals now prefer their tequila straight or in an effervescent, citrus cocktail called the "Paloma," which is Spanish for "dove." It is quite refreshing.

1 FRESH LIME, CUT INTO WEDGES

1 OUNCE TEQUILA

1 CAN (11.5 OZ.) FRESCA OR SQUIRT

CRACKED ICE

KOSHER SALT

Rub the rim of an 8 to 12 ounce glass with a lime wedge. Dip the rim of the glass into kosher or margarita salt, shaking off the excess salt. Fill the glass ¾ full with cracked ice. Pour in one shot of your favorite tequila, add a pinch of kosher salt, squeeze in the juice of a lime wedge, and toss the wedge into the glass. Fill the glass with Fresca or Squirt soda pop.

LOVE DOESN'T MAKE
THE WORLD GO 'ROUND.
LOVE IS WHAT MAKES THE RIDE
WORTHWHILE.

Cactus Colada

You don't have to be in Hawaii to taste a bit of tropical flavor! By replacing the rum with tequila and adding fresh lime, you start out with a piña colada, but finish up with a zing!
(Makes 4 servings)

½ CUP SWEETENED COCONUT FLAKES

½ CUP GOLD TEQUILA

½ CUP CREAM OF COCONUT MILK

1 CUP PINEAPPLE JUICE

JUICE OF 2 LIMES

3 TO 4 CUPS OF CRACKED ICE

Preheat oven to 350°F. Place the coconut flakes on a baking sheet and bake for 6 to 8 minutes, until lightly browned. Let cool completely. Meanwhile, combine the tequila, cream of coconut milk, pineapple juice, lime juice, and ice in a blender, and blend for 2 or 3 minutes, until the ice is smooth. Serve in 4 stemmed cocktail glasses. Sprinkle the coconut flakes on top.

HANG ONTO YOUR FAITH,
HOLD TIGHT TO YOUR FRIENDS.

Mexicana Gold

This cocktail has the hues of a western sunset. The blending of these different juices, tequila, and liqueur makes a luscious cocktail. This is my *Fiesta Mexicali* version of the tropical Mai Tai.
(Makes 1 serving)

1 ¼ OUNCES GOLD TEQUILA

¾ OUNCE ORANGE-FLAVORED LIQUEUR,
SUCH AS TRIPLE SEC, COINTREAU, OR GRAND MARNIER

1 ½ OUNCES PINEAPPLE JUICE

1 ½ OUNCES ORANGE JUICE

CRACKED ICE

SPLASH OF GRENADINE

1 LIME WEDGE

Pour the tequila, liqueur, pineapple juice, and orange juice into a shaker half filled with the cracked ice. Shake only a couple of times and pour into an Old-Fashioned glass half filled with cracked ice. Add grenadine and garnish with a lime wedge.

MAY YOU LIVE TO BE A HUNDRED YEARS
WITH ONE EXTRA YEAR TO REPENT.

Wine Whims

Even though many of my celebrations center around cervezas and the blending of margaritas, my *Fiesta Mexicali* fare and wine also complement each other nicely. Chiles and spices affect the taste of good wine, so pairing wines and spicy food is a very personal and individual experience.

Here are a few tips on matching wine and *Fiesta Mexicali* cuisine:
 • Fruity white wines, such as a Riesling, go well with spicy salsas, ceviches, and light seafood and chicken dishes.
 • Medium-bodied white wines, such as a California Chardonnay, go well with mild flavors such as my Green Chile Chicken Alfredo and Sopa de Lima.
 • Zinfandels go well with beef dishes such as Carne Asada, Classic Carnitas, Salpicon, and Sirlion Nachos.
 • Cabernets and Merlots are not as frequently paired with spicy foods. Many wine conissouiers claim that their rich taste clashes with the flavor of chile. However, popular Mexican restaurants around the country have started serving a variety of these dark red wines with milder chile dishes.

It is always best to offer your guests a variety of whites and reds. Develop your list of favorites by experimenting and tasting. And again, *Salud!*

Dulce de Leche Martini

The Dulce de Leche (pronounced Dool-say duh Le-chay), which means "sweet of milk" in Spanish, has been a popular candy in Latin America and Mexico for years. The small, chewy caramel squares were the inspiration for this seductively sweet caramel cocktail. (Makes 1 serving)

½ OUNCE GOOD-QUALITY RUM

CRACKED ICE

1 OUNCE HALF-AND-HALF CREAM

1 OUNCE CARAMEL SAUCE*

Pour the rum into a shaker half filled with cracked ice. Add the half-and-half cream and the caramel sauce. Shake well, and pour the liquid and the ice into a martini glass.

*I tried many caramel ice cream toppings, but Hershey's Classic Caramels Sundae Syrup gave the best flavor with a hint of salt to balance the sweetness.

Mexican Madras Martini

This summer martini is light with a fruity flavor. Infusing cranberry and orange juice gives a sweet foundation for this fun martini. (Makes 1 serving)

1 OUNCE TEQUILA

1 OUNCE ORANGE JUICE

1 OUNCE CRANBERRY JUICE

SPLASH OF FRESH LIME JUICE

CRACKED ICE

Pour the tequila, orange juice, cranberry juice, and lime juice into a shaker half filled with cracked ice. Shake well, and strain into a unique martini glass.

Millennium Martini

I developed this fabulous martini for a "martini night" at a local restaurant. This cocktail is stylish and sophisticated. (Makes 1 serving)

2 OUNCES GOOD-QUALITY VODKA

1 OUNCE RASPBERRY-FLAVORED LIQUEUR,

SUCH AS CHAMBORD

CRACKED ICE

SPLASH OF CRANBERRY JUICE

1 FRESH RASPBERRY, FOR GARNISH

Pour the vodka and liqueur into a shaker half filled with cracked ice. Shake, and strain into a chilled martini glass. Add the cranberry juice. Garnish with a single fresh raspberry on a fancy toothpick.

Melon Martini

This is the perfect cocktail for the daring cocktail maker! Try some new flavors; there are so many wonderful liqueurs on the market today. You will find blackberry, peach, and strawberry, just to name a few. (Makes 1 serving)

½ OUNCE TEQUILA

1 OUNCE MELON LIQUEUR, SUCH AS MIDORI*

½ OUNCE FRESH LIME JUICE

CRACKED ICE

Pour the tequila, liqueur, and lime juice into a shaker half filled with cracked ice. Shake well, and strain into a martini glass.

*I prefer using the Midori brand, because its striking emerald green color makes this a beautiful cocktail.

*This is my favorite "girlfriends" toast.
Do we believe it?
Naaah. Do we love it? Yes!*

WOMEN'S FAULTS ARE MANY.
MEN HAVE ONLY TWO:
EVERYTHING THEY SAY,
AND EVERYTHING THEY DO.

Fiesta Prioska

The tangy, bittersweet taste of this Brazilian cocktail is perfect for the fiery flavors of *Fiesta Mexicali* cuisine. High-quality vodka is essential for this light, refreshing drink. Smashing (or muddling) the rinds of the lime gives this drink its bittersweet twist. (Makes 1 serving)

1 TO 2 FRESH LIMES (DEPENDING ON SIZE)
2 TEASPOONS SUGAR
1½ OUNCES VODKA
2 CUPS CRACKED ICE

Quarter the lime. Place the lime quarters and the sugar in a rocks glass and mash with a wooden spoon or fork. Add the vodka, and pack the glass with 1 cup of the cracked ice. Pour into shaker, shake well, and strain back into the rocks glass. Top it with the remaining cracked ice, and let sit for 2 to 3 minutes before serving.

MAY OUR HOUSE
ALWAYS BE TOO SMALL TO HOLD
ALL OF OUR FRIENDS.

Frozen Tumbleweed

Dessert cocktails are a fun way to finish a meal. This blend of coffee- and chocolate-flavored liqueurs and ice cream is a rich treat. (Makes 4 servings)

3 OUNCES CHOCOLATE-FLAVORED LIQUEUR,
SUCH AS CRÉME DE CACAO
3 OUNCES COFFEE-FLAVORED LIQUEUR,
SUCH AS KAHLÚA
1 QUART GOOD-QUALITY VANILLA ICE CREAM
2 CUPS CRACKED ICE
WHIPPED CREAM (FOR GARNISH)

Pour the liqueurs and ice cream in a blender. Blend until smooth, about 2 to 3 minutes. Add the ice and blend for 2 to 3 minutes more, until slushy. Garnish with whipped cream. Serve in a wine glass.

MAY WE LIVE
TO LEARN WELL,
AND LEARN TO LIVE WELL.

Creamy Dreamy Orange Flurry

Remember the orange Popsicles filled with vanilla ice cream? Every summer we'd get them from the neighborhood ice cream truck. Well, try this frosty blend of peach and orange liqueurs and those memories will come flooding back. (Makes 4 servings)

3 OUNCES ORANGE-FLAVORED LIQUEUR,
SUCH AS TRIPLE SEC, COINTREAU, OR GRAND MARNIER
3 OUNCES PEACH SCHNAPPS
1 PINT GOOD-QUALITY VANILLA ICE CREAM
1 PINT ORANGE SHERBET
2 CUPS CRACKED ICE

Pour the liqueur, Peach Schnapps, and ice cream in a blender. Blend until smooth, about 2 to 3 minutes. Add ice and blend for 2 to 3 minutes more until slushy. Serve in a wine glass or an Old-Fashioned glass.

HERE'S TO ABSTINENCE—
AS LONG AS IT IS PRACTICED
IN MODERATION.

Sangria Spritzer

While on my quest for the perfect sangria recipe, my friend Sherley laughed at the thought of taking the time to mix wines, sugars, and fruit juices. She offered this simple recipe, and I have to say that it is the best and the quickest. So I proudly present the best sangria I have ever found, with the idea that less is best. (Makes 4 to 6 servings)

1 BOTTLE (750 ML.) RASPBERRY ZINFANDEL
4 CANS (11.5 OUNCES EACH) FRESCA
(NO OTHER BRAND WILL DO)
1 MEDIUM ORANGE, SLICED
1 MEDIUM LEMON, SLICED
1 LIME, SLICED
1 LIME, CUT IN HALF
CRACKED ICE

Combine the Zinfandel and the Fresca in a large glass pitcher. Add the orange, lemon, and lime slices. Squeeze juice from the lime halves into the sangria. Serve in Collins glasses half filled with ice.

TO OUR BEST FRIENDS,
WHO KNOW THE WORST ABOUT US,
BUT REFUSE TO BELIEVE IT.

Bloody Mary Bar

Anyone can fix a Bloody Mary, but creating a Bloody Mary bar gives your guests something to remember. This brunch-pleaser offers something for everyone. I start with a simple Bloody Mary mix, made with a favorite salsa, and then choose 4 to 6 garnishes and let my guests customize their own cocktails. (Makes 10 servings)

2 CUPS OF YOUR FAVORITE PICANTE-STYLE SALSA
1 CAN (1.36 LITERS) GOOD-QUALITY TOMATO JUICE
10 OUNCES GOOD-QUALITY VODKA
2 TABLESPOONS WORCESTERSHIRE SAUCE
1 TABLESPOON PREPARED HORSERADISH
CRACKED ICE

Puree the salsa in a blender until smooth. Combine the salsa puree and the tomato juice in a pitcher and chill. Pour 1 ounce of the vodka in a Collins glass half filled with cracked ice. Top with the tomato mixture. Add ½ teaspoon of the Worcestershire sauce and ¼ teaspoon of the horseradish in each Bloody Mary. Set out small bowls of any the following for garnishes:

WHOLE PICKLED GARLIC CLOVES	CHUNKS OF CUCUMBER
CRUSHED RED PEPPER FLAKES	FRESH GREEN ONIONS
CRACKED BLACK PEPPER	GREEK OLIVES
KOSHER SALT	PICKLED OKRA
GROUND CUMIN	MINCED CILANTRO
POWDERED GARLIC	A VARIETY OF HOT SAUCES
FRESH CELERY STALKS	FIESTA TOMATO RELISH (PAGE 12)
BABY DILL PICKLES	FRESH GREEN APPLE SLICES
FRESH YELLOW CHILES	(DIPPED IN LEMON JUICE TO
FRESH JALAPEÑOS	PREVENT DISCOLORING)
FRESH SNOW PEAS	GREEN CHILE,
FRESH SNAP PEAS	ROASTED AND CHOPPED

White Sangria

My sister Kate and I discovered this sangria with its citrus and apple garnish at the Aspen Food & Wine Classic a few years back. We rated this one top on that year's drink list.
(Makes 6 to 8 servings)

1 BOTTLE (750 ML.) EXTRA-DRY VERMOUTH

1 CUP ORANGE-FLAVORED LIQUEUR,

SUCH AS TRIPLE SEC, COINTREAU,

OR GRAND MARNIER

3 TABLESPOONS GRANULATED SUGAR

JUICE OF 3 ORANGES

JUICE OF 2 LEMONS

JUICE OF 2 LIMES

1 ORANGE, THINLY SLICED

1 LEMON, THINLY SLICED

1 LIME, THINLY SLICED

1 GRANNY SMITH APPLE, PEELED,

CORED, AND CUT INTO SMALL CHUNKS

8 OUNCES SPARKLING WATER

CRACKED ICE

Combine the Vermouth, liqueur, sugar, fruit juices, fruit slices, and apple chunks in a punch bowl or large pitcher. Mix well. Add sparkling water and cracked ice. Serve immediately.

To THE MEN I'VE LOVED,
To THE MEN I'VE KISSED,
MY HEARTFELT APOLOGIES
To THE MEN I'VE MISSED!

Sun-Kissed Tequila Tea

Around March you'll start seeing big jars of Sun Tea on the patios and walkways of the homes in Arizona. Sun Tea is popular in this hot spot of the country, and there is truly a distinctive taste in a tea that is brewed under the sun. I have infused that earthy flavor with tequila. For a fruitier and sweeter twist, add an Italian fruit syrup, which can be found in the coffee section of your grocery store.
(Makes 6 to 8 servings)

2 QUARTS SUN TEA*

1 CAN (12 OUNCES) FROZEN

LEMONADE CONCENTRATE, PREPARED AS DIRECTED

8 OUNCES GOLD TEQUILA, OR TO TASTE

2 LEMONS, SLICED

3 LIMES, SLICED

CRACKED ICE

½ CUP ITALIAN RASPBERRY OR

PEACH SYRUP (OPTIONAL)

Mix 2 quarts of Sun Tea with the lemonade and tequila in a large pitcher. Add the fruit slices. Serve over cracked ice in large goblets or tumblers. Or, for a sweeter Sun Tea, add 1 tablespoon of raspberry or peach Italian syrup to each glass before filling with ice, and then top with the Sun-Kissed Tequila Tea.

*To make 1 gallon of Sun Tea, place 3 family-sized tea bags in a 1-gallon jar. Fill with water, cover, and place in the warm sun for 2 to 3 hours. Remove the tea bags from the tea jar and serve.

Sunset Champagne

This lovely champagne cocktail dresses up any affair. I have served this simple punch at afternoon showers, brunches, and evening gatherings.
(Makes 6 to 8 servings)

2 BOTTLES (750 ML. EACH) CHAMPAGNE OR SPARKLING WINE

1 CUP PEACH SCHNAPPS

3 CANS (11.5 OUNCES EACH) PEACH NECTAR

GRENADINE

Combine the Champagne or sparkling wine, Schnapps, and nectar in a large punch bowl or serving bowl. Float a decorative frozen mold in the center*.
To serve, pour the punch in individual fluted champagne glasses, and add a splash of grenadine to each glass (it will settle to the bottom of the glass).

*To make the frozen mold, half fill a 6- to 8-inch round plastic bowl with water. Place a few orange slices and fresh raspberries (I use cranberries during the winter holidays) in the water, and carefully place in the freezer for 12 hours.

Los Tres Amigos!

Shooting tequila is a ritual we cherish in the West, but it's not for the faint of heart or the averse to alcohol. A little salt, a shot of tequila, and a little lime all add to the mystery of this spirit. These three friends are very popular in Mexico. Here is the proper methodology:

Line up your ingredients. Salt, tequila shot, lime wedge. Yell, "Uno, dos, tres!" Lick the area between your forefinger and thumb. Pour salt on the wet spot. Lick the salt and quickly drink (or "shoot") the tequila. Grab your lime wedge and bite into it, squeezing as much juice into your mouth as possible. Now pass the bottle.

Sun Devil Slammer

This little shot has a potent punch, but the freshness of the orange juice gives it a great flavor. (Makes 1 serving)

1 OUNCE GOLD TEQUILA
1 OUNCE FRESH SQUEEZED ORANGE JUICE
CRACKED ICE
2 LIME WEDGES

Pour the tequila and orange juice in a shaker half filled with cracked ice. Shake well. Strain into a shot glass. Squeeze the juice from 1 of the lime wedges into the glass. Quickly drink the tequila, orange juice, and lime mixture, and suck the juice out of the other lime wedge.

Mexican Mudslide

Mexican chocolate has a distinctive cinnamon taste to it. This blend of liqueurs comes together with the flavor of the cinnamon. (Makes 1 serving)

1 OUNCE COFFEE-FLAVORED LIQUEUR, SUCH AS KAHLUÁ
½ OUNCE CHOCOLATE-FLAVORED LIQUEUR,
SUCH AS CRÉME DE CACAO
1 OUNCE HEAVY CREAM
DASH OF CINNAMON

Pour the liqueurs and heavy cream into a shot glass or a martini glass. Sprinkle with a dash of cinnamon.

Woo Woo

This is a refreshing bit of heaven in a shot glass. The mellow flavor of the Schnapps accents the tartness of the cranberry juice. (Makes 1 serving)

⅓ OUNCE CRANBERRY JUICE
⅓ OUNCE GOOD-QUALITY VODKA
⅓ OUNCE PEACH SCHNAPPS

Pour the cranberry juice, vodka, and Schnapps into a shaker half filled with cracked ice. Shake well. Strain into a shot glass.

Fiesta Décor

A good Southwestern celebration creates a special kind of ambiance, and these are the parties I enjoy the most. They are the ones with a unique atmosphere—the ones with something in the air, a special background, a feeling you get as you walk in. Over the years I have watched, studied, and learned from the best party organizers. I found that when it comes to atmosphere, these party professionals all have two things in common: they know how to let their imaginations run wild, and they pay great attention to detail.

Now you can work some magic on your party, too. I've filled this chapter with a wide assortment of tips, suggestions, and my favorite creative projects. Some of them take a little time and a few dollars, but most of them are quick and incredibly easy. And because we are all so busy and rushed, I have even included a few fun ideas that I think of as "Grocery Store Décor." These are creative tips for your table that you can find in your local market while you are gathering your ingredients for a *Fiesta Mexicali* feast. Just begin well in advance of the party and have fun!

Desert Oasis

Mixing plants, cactus, and dried flowers will give your table a look of natural elegance. Simply select two or three lush green houseplants, place them in interesting baskets, and tuck Spanish moss around the edges. Group them together in the center of your table and adorn each plant with sprigs of small dried flowers or filler such as baby's breath or dried liatris. Run strands of raffia or ribbon between and around the baskets, and nestle small pots of cactus throughout the ribbon to finish off your table.

Authentic Table Coverings

A simple Mexican serape (a lightweight, colorfully woven piece of fabric) laid on top of a bright tablecloth is a fun, authentic touch for your table. Scrunch it up or lay it flat and place a centerpiece on top. If you are traveling through any tourist area in the Southwest along the Mexican border, it's easy to find an array of these multi-colored lightweight blankets.

Basketworks

Beautiful baskets are easy to find, and they have a way of giving your table an attractive flare. Try lining some large rustic baskets with bright tea towels, napkins, or fabric, and filling them with chips, bread, or tortillas. You can wrap utensils in bright napkins, tie them with raffia, and then place them in a basket on your serving table. Also, look for rectangular baskets to hold casserole dishes, or round baskets to use for serving a pot of beans. Place the serving dish in the basket, and then tuck brightly colored fabric around the serving dish to keep it warm and to fill in the space between the serving dish and the sides of the basket. Or, why not fill baskets with fresh fruits and veggies? For a summer gathering, place baskets of single fruit items on your serving table. A simple basket with a yellow print ribbon tied on the handle overflowing with lemons can be a real eye-catcher, or try a long breadbasket piled high with small green apples. In the fall, do the same with onions, garlic, squash, and chiles. Use your imagination, and especially your favorite local produce department.

Terra Cotta and Tile

✷

Don't throw out your old clay or ceramic pots! You can create a unique centerpiece with old terra cotta pots, and cracked or broken ones give an especially dramatic effect. Use the pots with a few 6 x 6-inch Spanish or Old World tiles from your local tile company. Place two or three medium-sized terra cotta clay pots on your table—some upright, one or two on their sides. Place plants such as English Ivy or Creeping Charlie in and around the pots. Cover the plant containers (if plastic) with Spanish moss by lightly gluing it to the containers. Then strategically place your tiles throughout, leaning some against clay pots, and using some as candleholders for four or five large (2 to 3 inches wide), rustic non-drip candles.

Coasters To Go

✷

The elegant coasters in the best kitchenware stores and catalogs can be made in a snap. Make them for your guests, for your host the next time you are invited out, or even for yourself. These are a simple Southwestern delight. Look for a variety of 4 x 4-inch deco tiles in rustic, Italian, Mediterranean, and Spanish styles at your local tile supplier or home-improvement center. They cost about $1 each for a simple design, and up to $5 each for an intricate hand-painted design. Use a 9 x 12-inch pre-cut square of felt, but because of the irregularities of each tile, you'll need to hold the felt up to the back of each tile. Clip the felt as close to the edge of each tile as possible. Place the tile face down, put glue across the center and in all four corners of the tile, and carefully press the felt onto the back of the tile, making sure the felt doesn't extend beyond the tile's edge. Let them dry for an hour. Stack and tie the coasters together with 4 or 5 strands of raffia or tulle (as shown). Start at the bottom of the stack and finish with a knot on top, and then do it again from the other direction. Finish with a bow on top.

Ristra!

Every autumn in New Mexico, just about a month after the chile harvest, stores and food stands display row after row of red chile ristras, which are 40 to 50 fresh red chiles strung together in a 2- to 3-foot strand. These brilliant red strands of hanging chiles make a spectacular sight. As they dry out, their color turns tones of rich earthy maroon and brown. Throughout the Southwest, it is customary to hang the ristras next to your front door to welcome guests, but you can also make a spectacular centerpiece by laying one large ristra or two small strands lengthwise in the center of your celebration table. Tuck bright silk or dried flowers such as sunflowers or Gerber daisies between the chiles. Tie a large raffia bow, using 8 to 10 strands of raffia about 2 to 3-feet long, at the hanging end of the ristra, or where the two ristras meet if using two smaller ones. Arrange the display in the center of your table.

Unusual Objects, Unusual Comments

✳

An old clock, a pair of kid's cowboy boots, a few old books, a couple of interesting vases—these are just a few unusual objects that you can work into table toppers. For example, you can fill a child's cowboy boot with dried flowers or lay a stack of old books about Mexican history under a plant. Arrange and cluster the items with candles, fresh flowers, or lush green plants, and you can create interesting conversational centerpieces for your table.

Mexican Canned-Goods Garden

✳

This is really Grocery Store Décor. Go through your local market's Mexican food section and find the Mexican canned goods printed in Spanish. They are generally bright and colorful and will be full of jalapeños, hominy, menudo, etc. You will find gallon, quart, and pint-sized cans. Buy 6 or 8 cans in a variety of sizes, empty the contents into resealable plastic bags, and either use the food for your party or call and ask to donate it to a local soup kitchen. Rinse each can well before using. Select various sizes of fresh potted mums and green plants, and place or re-pot in each can. Tuck Spanish moss around the edges of each plant. Insert sprigs of dried flowers such as baby's breath to pull all the plants together in a group for your table.

Mexican Pewter and Hand-Blown Glassware

✳

Mexican pewter and hand-blown glassware carry the traditions of authentic entertaining. Both can be bought almost anywhere these days. Mexican pewter (a molded aluminum imported from Mexico) has become a hot decorating item; its rustic silver appearance adds a casual dimension to your celebration. Whether you obtain casserole-holders for Pyrex baking dishes or small, silver bowls to hold spicy salsas, they are inexpensive and usually ovenproof. I've collected quite a few serving pieces that always come in handy. And hand-blown glasses, usually imported from Mexico, make a margarita or glass of sangria much more fun. You will find a variety of colors these days, rimmed in blues and greens, and sometimes multicolored. The pitchers and bowls are also wonderful accent pieces for your table. Check the resources on page 117 for more information.

Glassware Affair

✳

As you shop flea markets, second-hand stores, and garage sales, collect an array of interesting goblets, dessert glasses, and wine glasses. You will find a variety of shapes, colors, and sizes. Arrange your unique collection on a silver tray for a stunning look. Remember, your wildest cocktail is even more exciting when served in an unusual glass.

Fiesta Napkin Rings

✷

I love this authentic look! Cornhusks are traditionally used for wrapping tamales, but these simple little napkins rings really add to your Fiesta Mexicali celebration and cost only pennies. A 6-ounce bag of cornhusks will make up to 35 napkin rings; you will need one cornhusk for each napkin ring. As there will always be some cornhusks that don't work, start with a few extras.

1. Soak the cornhusks in warm water for at least 30 minutes until they are pliable.
2. While the remaining cornhusks are still soaking, take one out and lay it on a flat surface with the pointed end towards you.
3. Starting from top to bottom, gently pull away the sides of the cornhusk, one side at a time, until you are left with a width of 3 inches across the top (the bottom will still be pointed).
4. Fold the whole left side inwards (about an inch at the top) and then repeat with the right side.
5. Gently wrap this strip of cornhusk around the neck of a bottle to form a 1-inch diameter circle (about the size of a salad-dressing bottle).
6. Slide the cornhusk circle off the top of the bottle and use paperclips to hold the cornhusk in that shape (3 or 4 clips per cornhusk).
7. Place the wet cornhusk on a flat surface for approximately 2 hours to dry.
8. Repeat these steps until you have the desired amount of napkin rings.
9. After the rings are dry, gently slide them over a 15 x 17 inch napkin that has been folded lengthwise.
10. Tie a piece of raffia around the outside of each ring into a decorative bow, and trim the ends.

Welcome Wreath

✳

A festive wreath laced with bright ribbons looks great with delicate tin ornaments handmade in Mexico. You can do this project in just a couple of hours, and your results will be well worth the time. A friend and I lined her front walkway with the Jeweled Glass Lights described on page 107 and hung this beautiful wreath on her front door. What an entrance!

To make this wreath, place an 18- to 20-inch vine wreath (found at your local hobby store) on a counter. Using a hot-glue gun, lightly glue each of 6 strands of ribbon (each ¼ inch wide and 2½ feet long in assorted vivid colors) around the front surface of the wreath. Start at one side of the wreath and glue the ribbon down by placing a dot of glue on the underside of the ribbon and pressing it to the wreath about every 4 inches, zig-zagging around the face of the wreath, until you have glued the entire ribbon around the wreath. Repeat this step with each color ribbon. Use three shorter (10-inch) ribbons for hanging tin ornaments on the inside of the wreath. Check the resource list on page 117 for information on where to find tin ornaments.

El Natural Table Linens

⁂

Pull your celebration centerpieces together with splashes of color. If you can't seem to find what you want in color and style for your table, just create your own! Select a 100 percent cotton fabric. Your table runner should be 15 inches wide and as long as your table plus 26 inches. Turn up a quarter-inch hem all the way around your cut fabric. Iron it, and then turn the unfinished edges up another quarter inch. You can either stitch it with your sewing machine, or use a narrow interfacing and iron the finished edge around your runner. You can also use a 2 x 4-foot piece of brightly colored, coordinating fabric to scrunch up and place on top of your runner. It will be the focal point of your celebration table.

Bright, colorful paper napkins are always appropriate for casual gatherings, but if you want a special touch that coordinates with your table linens, create your own fabric napkins without any sewing. Choose brightly colored Southwest prints or solids. Create a pattern by cutting out a 15 x 17-inch rectangle (the size of the napkins) using tissue paper.

Lightweight cotton fabrics work the best and wash well. One yard of 45-inch wide fabric is enough for four 15 x 17-inch napkins. Simply spread out your fabric, place your pattern one-half inch from the fold, cut out the pattern with sharp pinking shears, and then repeat. I like the casual look that you get from frayed edges. If they fray or unravel, just clip the longer threads.

Sharing Recipes and Toasts

⁂

Make copies of the recipes you are using for your party, and then roll them up and tie them with a ribbon. Place them in a festive bowl near your food serving area. As your guests compliment you on the wonderful food, share your recipes with them. Take it a step farther by making copies of a favorite toast to send home with your guests, perhaps rolled, tied, and placed in a glass bowl by the front door.

Jeweled Glass Lights

❋

I love to scatter light sources around a party. They are romantic and full of color. Take a small 6-inch round glass vase about 4 inches high. Your local hobby store will have these. Cut a sheet of colored tissue paper into a 17 x 17-inch square. Place the vase in the center of the tissue and bring up all the edges to the rim of the vase. Secure the tissue to the rim with a couple of strands of raffia tied in a bow. Place a votive candle in the vase, and light it. Make sure the corners of the tissue paper are arranged away from the opening of the vase so they do not burn. Place these little jewels on the serving table, in the kitchen, on a coffee table, near the drinks, or in the entry.

Fiesta Musica

Live Mariachi or Musical Performers

I live in a community that cherishes Mexican, Latino, and Salsa music. These sounds have everything to do with food, family, friends, and celebrating. A mariachi group or trio of singers adds an authentic tone to your celebration. With a little research and networking, you can find great-sounding groups. Contact your community cultural center or the music department at your local university. Even our local high schools have mariachi groups that perform for private functions. Ask about an upcoming event where such a group will be playing, and then go check them out.

Latin and Southwestern Rhythms

Latino, Mexican, and Salsa music is romantic, sensual, and exciting. It adds a rhythmic fusion that unites so many cultures. Start a collection of great Salsa or Latino music. There are so many classics, and this music never goes out of style. Check your local music store, which will almost certainly have a Salsa or Latino section. There, you will find easy listening, on the edge rock, strolling mariachi, and serious dance tunes. So take your time and ask to listen to the variety available. Several popular names to look for are the Gipsy Kings, Gloria Estefan, and Los Tri-O. I just picked up 3 new CDs that are perfect for a Fiesta Mexicali affair: Los Doctores Del Rimo, Franki Negron (Por tu Placer), and Olga Tanon (Yo Por Ti). Consider making your party interactive by hiring a dance instructor to teach your guests how to "Salsa dance." Check with your local dance studios or contact the dance departments at your local high school, community college, or university. It's great fun, and you will definitely create a night to remember.

Luminarias

There is no candle-keeper simpler to make than the Southwest luminaria, a traditional Christmas light and a sweet addition to any party. The feeling of warmth and romance that these lights offer is indescribable. Simply place 2 cups of sand in a small, lunch-size brown paper bag, fold down the top edge of the bag one inch, taking care to keep the paper away from the flame, and place a votive candle inside. Line your front walkway and porch with the luminarias to welcome your guests. Create an intimate atmosphere on the patio or under the stars with luminarias and lush green plants. I use a few luminarias indoors as well on my hearth, in the bathroom, and on my serving table. I like to decorate each one with a little ribbon and a few dried flowers.

Old-Fashioned Lanterns

A patio party looks wonderful with a few lanterns flickering as centerpieces or as part of your serving-table décor. These lanterns are fun and easy to create. Simply paint the dish part of a terra cotta flowerpot (the clay saucer that you place the flowerpot on to catch the water). Use a saucer that is about 6 ¾ inches in diameter. Paint it a bright color, such as red, orange, or turquoise, and let it dry. Using a fine-point brush, highlight each saucer with Aztec, Indian, and Mexican designs such as zigzags, triangles, crosses, or any other Southwestern doodles you can come up with. Light your candle and allow the wax to drip into the center of the clay dish. Before the wax dries, place the candle upright in the wax to secure it. Gently pour sand into the dish around the candle. Place a hurricane lamp over the candle and push it gently down into the sand.

Raffia and Ribbon

❖

Raffia and ribbon can really pull everything together for a celebration.

• Roll up your silverware in bright paper or fabric napkins, tie with raffia, and arrange in a large (10- to 12-inch) clay flowerpot. Tie another big raffia bow around the edge of your flowerpot.

• Tightly tie 3 inches of brightly colored wire ribbon in a knot around the stem of each margarita glass and place the glasses on a large colorful tray.

• Tie a fun, 6- to 8-inch wire ribbon bow on the handle of a serving pitcher used to serve the drink of the night.

• Tie a large bow on your front doorknob, using approximately 10 strands of raffia, each 2- to 3-feet long.

• Tie 7 to 10 strands of raffia around each bath towel (the ones your guests won't be using) hanging on your bathroom towel rack.

• Wire ribbon bows create a warm, happy feeling, so tie them on doorknobs, pillows, stair railings, lights, chandeliers, barstools, and the backs of chairs. Bows can go anywhere.

Balloons

❖

Atmosphere often means coziness, and that often means filling up spaces to bring all your guests together as a single group. I have found that brightly colored balloons are an excellent way to heighten the level of excitement for your gathering. Here are three ways to arrange balloons, all of which can lend a whimsical look to your room: randomly scatter non-helium balloons in the corners on the floor; tie helium balloons in clusters around the edges of the party, on the backs of chairs, and to the legs of end tables; or (assuming the ceiling isn't too high), float helium balloons to the ceiling with a ribbon tied to each one, just long enough to dangle over your guests' heads.

Banners

❖

A banner with a central theme unites and sets the tone for your gathering. Take a phrase or title from a song or poem, or use a great line from a movie. (Some possibilities: "Born to Be Wild!" "We are Family!" "We Will, We Will Rock You!") At a recent class reunion, our committee chose a Rod Stewart song entitled "Forever Young." We had a sign company print it on a banner in bright colors. It was hung low enough at the entrance of the party so that every guest entering could stop and sign it with brightly colored markers that we had supplied.

Signature Spirits

Chile Pepper Spice

2 TO 3 RED BELL PEPPERS,
SEEDED AND SLICED INTO
STRIPS 1-INCH WIDE
2 TO 3 SERRANO CHILES
1 TO 2 YELLOW CHILES
1 TO 3 FRESH JALAPEÑOS
1 RED ONION, THINLY SLICED AND SEPARATED
1 TO 4 SPRIGS FRESH ROSEMARY
10 TO 12 OUNCES HIGH QUALITY VODKA
1 12-OUNCE JAR OR 2 6-OUNCE JARS, WITH LIDS

Poke holes in the jalapeños and small chiles with a fork; this will help the infusion process. Layer the bell peppers, chiles, onion, and rosemary in the jars. Fill each jar up as much as possible, making sure they are full. Fill the jars with vodka and cover with a lid. Attach a bow with instructions to remove the veggies from the jar within 2 days to prevent fermenting, as well as a little note that says: "Serve with your favorite Bloody Mary Mix."

Citrus Kiss

2 TO 3 LEMONS AND LIMES,
WASHED, SEEDED, AND SLICED
SIMPLE SYRUP (SEE RECIPE BELOW)
6 TO 8 OUNCES VODKA
1 12-OUNCE JAR OR 2 6-OUNCE JARS, WITH LIDS

Simple syrup is, well, simple to make. Just combine equal parts water and sugar in a saucepan, bring to a boil, and stir to dissolve sugar. Let cool. Refrigerate up to 2 weeks.

Place the sliced lemons and limes in the jars, half-fill each with Simple Syrup, top with vodka, and cover with a lid. Attach a bow with instructions to remove the fruit from the jar within 2 days to prevent fermenting, as well as a little note that says "Serve on the rocks, mix with club soda, or add Collins mix."

Veggie and Fruit Fiesta

✳

Speaking of the produce department, create a fresh-produce centerpiece by separating, washing, and drying the leaves of a head of romaine lettuce. Place a piece of plastic, about 12 by 16 inches, in the center of your celebration table and arrange the lettuce leaves in the center of the plastic. Then arrange colorful squash, eggplant, tomatoes, zucchini, garlic, chiles, and onions in an elaborate display. Arrange the largest items first, and then tuck the smaller ones in and around the others. Use bunches of fresh herbs such as parsley and cilantro to fill in little gaps and pull this fresh centerpiece together. Flowers and fresh produce are my favorite combination for table décor.

Another idea is to place fresh lemon and lime slices in a clear vase, fill it with water, and then arrange fresh-cut flowers such as daisies or daffodils in it. Or, for a really unique floral arrangement, you can create a great base out of baby carrots, little fresh chiles, or sliced oranges. Just fill any clear glass container three-quarters full with colorful produce, add water to cover, and then gently arrange your favorite flowers—roses, carnations, daisies, lilies—in the jar, and add a coordinating wire ribbon or a few strands of raffia tied in a bow.

Hand-Painted Glasses

✳

What a great little memento for your guests! Pick up inexpensive clear shot glasses, margarita glasses, or martini glasses at your local restaurant supply house or discount store. Paint colorful designs or the date of your party on each glass. Look at your local hobby store for paint specifically intended for decorating glassware, and then use the paint to create simple but elegant designs for your guests. It's a treasure they can use again and again.

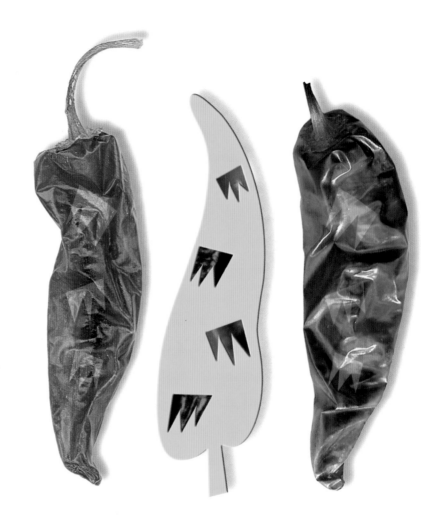

Resources

Mexican Tableware, Ornaments, & Linens

ANTIQUA DE MEXICO
3235 W. Orange Grove Road
Tucson, Arizona 85704
www.mexicanmart.com

AZ TRADING POST
822 East Union Hills Drive
PMB #102
Phoenix, Arizona 85024
www.aztradingpost.com

BAZAAR DEL MUNDO
Design Center Accessories
2754 Calhoun Street
San Diego, CA 92110
619/296-3161
Artes De Mexico Shop
619/296-3266
www.bazaardelmundo.com

GALERIA ON THE PLAZA
P.O. Box 1017
Mesilla, New Mexico 88046
505/526-9771

JACKALOPE
INTERNATIONAL
2820 Cerrillos Road
Santa Fe, New Mexico 87505
505/471-8539
or
834 Hwy. 44
Bernalillo, NM 87004
505/867-9813
www.jackalopeinternational.com

PICAFLOR
206 South 1st Avenue
Yuma, Arizona 85364
928/782-6535

PIER ONE IMPORTS
800/245-4595
www.pierone.com

STAHMANN'S
COUNTRY STORE
22505 South Highway 28
San Miguel, NM 88058
800/654-6887
www.stahmanns.com

TLAQUEPAQUE
3120 East Bell Road
Phoenix, Arizona 85032
602/485-5858

Fresh Green and Red Chile

BUENO BRAND PRODUCTS
2001 4th Street NW
Albuquerque, NM 87102
800/888-7336
505/243-2722
www.buenofoods.com

HATCH CHILE EXPRESS
622 Franklin
Hatch, New Mexico 87937
800/292-4454
www.hatch-chile.com

RISTRAMNN CHILE
COMPANY
2531 Avenida de Mesilla
Las Cruces, NM 88005
505/526-8667

Index

Acknowledgments

My most heartfelt "thank you" goes to two people who made this book a reality: first, to my agent, Lisa Ekus, who recognized my desire to write and cook for others and guided me through this experience, encouraging me and calming the storms all along the way; and second, to Ken Bookman, for his wonderful ability to make everything sound better and for keeping me focused. It has been a pleasure.

I also want to thank Eric Pearson, Dennis Quintana, and the crew at News Channel 9 in El Paso for believing in me and allowing me to share my "7-ingredient/30-minute" recipes with the viewers of West Texas and southern New Mexico every week since 1998. You guys are the best!

To my Publisher, Dave Jenney, and my Editor, Tammy Gales, thank you for believing in me and my *Mexicali* cuisine. I would also like to thank my book designer, Lanie Schwichtenberg, and my food stylists, Cathy Marshall and Judy Reynolds, for their creative talents. And, of course, a big thank you goes to the talented Christopher Marchetti.

There are many other very important people who have influenced me and contributed in some way to the creation of this book. First, I want to thank my dear mother, Fran Cleary, for stressing the importance of simplicity in the kitchen and taking advantage of shortcuts whenever possible. Thanks, Mom, I love ya! A big hug to Louise Braden, Liney Jessen, and Polly Coffeen for stressing the importance of entertaining for those you love. A huge "thank you" to Dan Coffeen for the opportunity to experience the different cultures and cuisines around the Southwest. Thank you to my dear friend Tara Sheffield for giving me an awareness of faith and a circle of inspirational friends. "Cheers" to Cynthia Gallagher for lots of laughs during our cocktail analysis sessions! A warm thank you to Sherley and Jeff O'Brien for their hospitality and deep discussions about chiles, liqueurs, and crafts. Thank you, Donna and Clint Curry for your generous spirit and recipe tips. To Sally Stahmann Rovirosa, Beverly Hart, and the gang at Stahmann Farms, thanks for being there when I needed you all! Thank you to the members of St. Paul's Methodist Church for giving me a prayerful beginning and a thankful end to each week during this writing process.

Finally, a huge "thank you" to all my girlfriends, neighbors, and family, for watching my kids, sampling my food, and giving me your honest opinions.

KELLEY CLEARY COFFEEN
was born and raised in the Southwest.
She is the author of the self-published
Great College Cookbook of the Southwest,
which was featured on "Good Morning America."
As a home economist, Kelley enjoys sharing time-saving tips
and lifestyle management ideas on her weekly television segment
"Kelley's Kitchen." She lives in Las Cruces, New Mexico with her family.